2003

Differentiated Instructional Strategies

for Writing
in the Content
Areas

Differentiated Instructional Strategies
for Writing
in the Content
Areas

Carolyn Chapman • Rita King

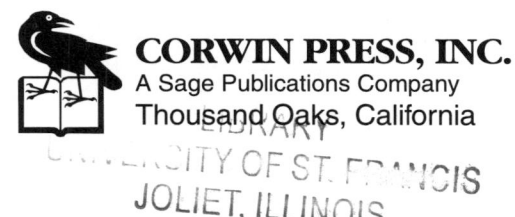

CORWIN PRESS, INC.
A Sage Publications Company
Thousand Oaks, California

For information:

Corwin Press, Inc.
A Sage Publications Company
2455 Teller Road
Thousand Oaks, California 91320
www.corwinpress.com

Sage Publications Ltd.
6 Bonhill Street
London EC2A 4PU
United Kingdom

Sage Publications India Pvt. Ltd.
B-42 Panchsheel Enclave
Post Box 4109
New Delhi 110 017 India

Printed in the United States of America

Library of Congress Cataloging-in-Publication Data

Chapman, Carolyn, 1945-
Differentiated instructional strategies for writing in the content areas /
Carolyn Chapman and Rita King.
     p. cm.
Includes bibliographical references and index.
ISBN 0-7619-3826-5 (cloth) -- ISBN 0-7619-3827-3 (pbk.)
    1. English language-Composition and exercises-Study and teaching.
2. Language arts-Correlation with content subjects. 3. Individualized instruction.
I. King, Rita M. II. Title.
LB1576.C419 2003
372.62'3--dc21

                                              2002155469

This book is printed on acid-free paper.

03 04 05 06 10 9 8 7 6 5 4 3 2 1

Acquisitions editor:	Faye Zucker
Editorial assistant:	Juli Parnell
Production editor:	Sanford Robinson
Copy editor:	Pam Suwinsky
Typesetter:	C&M Digitals (P) Ltd.
Proofreader:	Toni Williams
Cover designer:	Tracy Miller
Indexer:	Teri Greenberg

Contents

Every teacher is a writing teacher. In the differentiated writing classroom, teachers work with each student's unique needs. All students learn to apply information, to think and write critically, to think and write creatively, and to solve problems in their world. These skills develop self-directed learners and confident writers.

In the differentiated writing classroom, teachers create environments that motivate and challenge the student writer while also providing a safe and positive environment that instills self-efficacy. Assessing the classroom climate for writing includes finding the right spot for each student's Write Spot.

In the differentiated writing classroom, students learn the value of writing to inform and to express important ideas in the real world. Teachers work with student writers in all learning styles and multiple intelligences, recognizing the many developmental stages of each writer, which may include Scribbling, Picture Making, Storytelling, Letter Shaking, Copying, Sound Making, Sentence Making, and Story Making. Invented spelling is an important component of writing in the content areas during many of these developmental stages of writing.

Teachers in the content areas who assign writing tasks are often the first to observe student writing problems and the many different writing personalities, behaviors, and feelings students bring to their writing assignments and formal assessments. Checklists, rubrics, scales, surveys, open-ended questions, portfolios, conferences, and Sixteen Words for the Wise can be helpful prescriptions when writing problems are diagnosed.

Flexible grouping is an essential strategy in the differentiated writing classroom. Students can immerse themselves in the craft of writing descriptive, expository, persuasive, or narrative essays as part of the Total group (T), Alone (A), with a Partner (P), or within a Small group (S). The effective teacher TAPS into student writing talent through each step of the writing process from Prewriting through First Draft, Revision, Editing, Final Copy, and Publication.

Research shows that new and unique experiences improve the brain's ability to store and to retrieve information. Teachers who use differentiated writing strategies strategically and explicitly find that novelty is an effective motivational tool to use with content information because it generates excitement and enjoyment in the learning process. Writing strategies include use of varying styles and genres, personification, brainstorming, "jump start" prompts, journals, research, note taking, outlines, rubrics, essays, rhymes and riddles, poetry, text characters, and forty Writing from A to Z tips that develop learners with focused attention and an eager approach to writing activities.

Teachers make a difference in the writing journey of each life they touch. Effective writing teachers in the differentiated classroom use Choice Boards, Agendas, and Lesson Plans designed to meet each student's individual needs before, during, and after the writing experience. Effective writing teachers develop and support young authors whose writing skills last a lifetime.

Acknowledgments

The authors extend deep appreciation to the following educators who have assisted and inspired us through our writing of this book: Lisa Bogle, Nancy Bradshaw, Debbie Seigfreid, Liz Bennett, Sarah Jackson, Joan Clark Mann, Marti Richardson, Terri Stumpf, and Jim Chapman.

A very special thank you to Jim Chapman. His support sustained and encouraged us in this writing journey.

Faye Zucker's vivacity, advice and confidence gave us the writing wings to soar.

Corwin Press thanks the following reviewers for their contributions to this volume:

Nancy Creech, Roseville, MI

Ann Fulk, Fairfax Station, VA

Stacy Kasse, Cherry Hill, NJ

Joann Sherman, Northridge, CA

About the Authors

Carolyn Chapman continues her life's goal as an international educational consultant, author, and teacher. She supports educators in their process of change for today's students. She has taught in kindergarten to college classrooms. Her interactive, hands-on professional development opportunities focus on challenging the mind to ensure success for learners of all ages. All students *do* learn. Why not take control of that learning by putting excitement and quality in effective learning? Carolyn walks her walk and talks her talk to make a difference in the journey of learning in today's classrooms.

Carolyn authored *If the Shoe Fits . . . How to Develop Multiple Intelligences in the Classroom* and *Sail Into Differentiated Instruction*. She has co-authored *Multiple Assessments for Multiple Intelligences, Multiple Intelligences Through Centers and Projects, Differentiated Instructional Strategies for Reading in the Content Areas, Differentiated Instructional Strategies: One Size Doesn't Fit All,* and *Test Success in the Brain Compatible Classroom*. Video Journal of Education, Inc., features Carolyn Chapman in Differentiated Instruction. Carolyn's company, Creative Learning Connection, Inc., has also produced a CD, *Carolyn Chapman's Making the Shoe Fit*. Each of these publications demonstrates Carolyn's desire and determination to make an effective impact for educators and students. She may be contacted through the Creative Learning Connection Web site at www.carolynchapman.com.

Rita King is an adjunct professor in the Department of Educational Leadership at Middle Tennessee State University. She has more than twenty years of teacher-training experience. As principal and director of the university's teacher-training program in the laboratory school, she taught methods courses and conducted demonstration lessons. Rita's doctorate degree is in Educational Leadership. Her formal training (Ed.D, Ed.S., M.A., and B.S.) has been directly related to education and teacher training.

As an international consultant, Rita conducts training sessions for teachers, administrators, and parents on local, state, and international levels. Her areas of expertise include multiple intelligences, practical applications of brain-based research, differentiated learning, reading and writing strategies, creating effective learning environments, and strategies for test success. Rita's sessions give educators and parents innovative, engaging activities to develop students as self-directed, independent learners. Participants enjoy Rita's practical, easy-to-use strategies, sense of humor, enthusiasm, and genuine desire to foster the love of learning. She may be contacted through the Creative Learning Connection Web site at www.carolynchapman.com or kingrs@bellsouth.net

Rita co-authored *Test Success in the Brain Compatible Classroom* and *Differentiated Instructional Strategies for Reading in the Content Areas.*

Introduction

Infusing Writing in the Content Areas

The Author's Flight

A young author develops writing wings.
Each takes a unique learning journey.
Each one writes the best that he can.
Why compare one against the other?
Each writer is unique. Each passage is special.
Each author's flight is limitless.

—Adapted from "A Butterfly in the Wind"

Each student is a writer. Each writer has diverse unique needs. To meet these needs the teacher can differentiate the content, the instructional strategies and activities, the assessment tools, and the performance tasks (Gregory and Chapman, 2001). The way each teacher influences the student's use of the writing craft will affect the learner's writing destiny.

Effective writing teachers know how students learn. They pre-assess, so their students' strengths, abilities, and interests are used strategically to plan successful writing experiences. Teachers choose strategies that jog the learner's mind with higher-order thinking skills and creativity. Deeper thinking is stimulated with the use of open-ended questions.

The guidelines, expectations, and evaluation procedures for each activity are explained clearly. Routine feedback with appropriate guidance is provided. Writers are led to see errors as opportunities for improvement. All writing attempts are supported. Each success is genuinely praised with specific feedback.

Effective teachers present writing as a tool for learning and expressing ideas. They share various forms of writing with their students to model and illustrate the purposes and the pleasures that come from content mastery and authorship.

The written word is used more today than ever before. Individuals are no longer passive, but instead are active communicators, using electronic tools including e-mail and faxes. Writing is a key form of communication. Students *must* know how to write. It is essential!

Teachers are required to infuse writing in all content areas. In every classroom, the teacher expects students to have a pencil and paper. Every instructor who gives writing assignments is a writing teacher. For example, in the math classroom, students write out step-by-step procedures for a solution to a problem. In the language arts classroom, the teacher asks students to write an essay. The teacher models the expectations of a writer daily in classrooms in each grade level and content area.

Open-ended questions are given on tests. Often students know the information and can explain it to their peers. They bog down, however, when they try to get their thoughts on paper. The student must be taught, "If I can say it, I can write it." When this approach is one of the established expectations for the "way we do things around here," students perform better and show what they know.

A major goal of education is for students to become self-directed learners as thinkers and productive problem solvers. Differentiated instruction meets this need because each aspect of the individual is considered, including the learner's intelligences, learning styles, and emotional states. "Differentiation is a philosophy that enables teachers to plan strategically in order to reach the needs of diverse learners in classrooms today" (Gregory & Chapman, 2001, p. x).

In the differentiated writing classroom, teachers work with each student's unique needs. Goals for each learner are

- To know how to apply information
- To think and write critically
- To think and write creatively
- To solve problems in the real world

These skills develop self-directed learners and confident authors.

We developed this resource to provide writing strategies and skills for educators to use with textbook information and related sources. We believe each idea, strategy, and activity can be used to assist learners in the diverse ways they process information for long-term memory, test success, and everyday use.

TURN ON THE WRITER

Most toddlers find joy in holding a pencil in their hands. After a few years, however, many students respond to writing activities and assignments as dreaded experiences. Why do these negative feelings exist? We believe

Figure 0.1   Tools and Strategies for Infusing Writing in the Differentiated Classroom

Creating a Climate for Writing	*Knowing the Writer*	*Diagnosing and Assessing Writers*	*Differentiating the Writing Process*	*Instructional Strategies and Activities*	*Curriculum Approaches*
Writing Environment ❖ Writers are authors ❖ Non-threatening ❖ Open ❖ Accepting	**Stages of a Writer** • Scribbler • Picture Maker • Storyteller • Letter Shaker • Copier • Sound Maker • Sentence Maker • Story Maker	**Knowing the Authors** ⋗ Drawing Dana ⋗ Insecure Inez ⋗ Lollygagging Lonnie ⋗ Stumped Stan ⋗ Wordy Wilma ⋗ Author Arthur	**Flexible Grouping** ❖ **T** Total Group ❖ **A** Alone ❖ **P** Partner ❖ **S** Small Group	**Formats and Genres** **Personification** **Writing Strategies** ⋗ Brainstorming ⋗ Journaling ⋗ Note Taking ⋗ Model adjustable adjustment curriculum compacting problem-based project development	**Approaches** ⋏ Choice Boards ⋏ Agendas ⋏ Contracts
Razzmatazz to Thingamajigs ⋏ Cool Tools ⋏ Material Magic ⋏ Ready References	**Writing and the Brain** • Memory • Flow • Metacognition	**Tools for Diagnosis and Assessment**	**Types of Writing** ⋏ Descriptive ⋏ Expository ⋏ Persuasive ⋏ Narrative	⋏ Writing Essays ⋏ Poetry Adaptations	
The Write Spot	**Learning Styles**	**Questioning** ⋏ Open-Ended Questions ⋏ Choices ⋏ Sixteen Words for the Wise	**The Writing Process** ⋏ Getting Started: Prewriting ⋏ Sloppy Copy: First Draft ⋏ Hamming It Up: Revision ⋏ Tuning It Up: Editing ⋏ Neat Sheet: Final Copy ⋏ Publishing: Sharing and Celebrating	**Getting to Know Text Characters** **Writing from A to Z**	
Provide Choices	**Multiple Intelligences** • Verbal/Linguistic • Musical/Rhythmic • Logical/Mathematical • Visual/Spatial • Bodily/Kinesthetic • Naturalist • Intrapersonal • Interpersonal	**Portfolios** ❖ Gathering Information ❖ Conferences			
Motivational Strategies • Internal motivation • Instill self-efficacy • Develop self requested learners • Presexualized Learning	**Sternberg's Triarchy** • Practical • Analytical • Creative			**Lesson Planning** **Effective Authors**	

3

many students receive negative feedback through grades and informal comments from teachers. They become convinced that they cannot write. These authors build barriers to writing experiences because they fear failure.

Long, boring assignments "turn off" the student's desire to write. The student hears, "Answer the questions at the end of the chapter," or "Write the list of words and the definitions." These writing assignments make a student think this work is the "same old, same old thing." It is a shame that the student's natural desire to write is turned off so easily. Teachers need to be aware of students' emotional barriers and "turn on" their writing enthusiasm. Each experience is planned so the student visualizes himself as a successful, productive writer. Attitude Is Altitude!

Figure 0.1 provides teachers with an overview of ways to select writing tools and strategies that meet the authors' needs and enrich the content information.

Use Hooks as Motivational Strategies

The word *hook* refers to one or more motivational strategies designed to focus students' attention, to intrigue them, and to stimulate their desire to learn more about the topic or skill.

Adapt Each Writing Strategy or Activity to the Learner's Needs

Each activity and strategy in this resource may be adapted to an individual learner's needs. As the learning director, the teacher must consider each student's diverse needs and levels of understanding to make appropriate adaptations.

- Add one or more steps to the activity to clarify procedures.
- Remove one or more steps to simplify the guidelines or assignment.
- Replace the terminology with words the student understands.
- Extend the activity by providing or assigning creative experiences.
- Challenge the learner's mind by adding experiences that involve higher-order thinking skills.
- Use the activity for the total group *(T)*, for a student working alone *(A)*, for partner work *(P)*, or for small groups *(S)*—TAPS.

Focus on Thinking

In many classrooms, educators emphasize writing mechanics and the "look" of the work. Writing involves complex problem-solving techniques, so more emphasis should be placed on getting the information on paper.

The most valuable aspects of each writing experience are the content, the organization, and the author's style as an effective communicator.

EVERY TEACHER IS A WRITING TEACHER: THE POWER IS YOURS!

Every class has writing assignments. It is not realistic for a teacher to say, "This is *not* a writing class! These students should learn writing skills in language arts classes!" or, "If they have not learned the writing skills by now, they are not capable of learning them." All educators must assume these challenges.

Teachers need to take an inventory of their personal feelings related to teaching young writers. According to Marjorie Frank in *If You're Trying to Teach Kids How to Write . . . You've Gotta Have This Book!* (1995, p. 19) teachers need to understand their "attitudes and beliefs, fears and abilities." An individual's self-efficacy, or belief in his success as a teacher, will impact the way writing activities are approached. Teachers have the power to change the quality of students' lives by giving them the writing skills they need for academic and personal success.

Figure 0.2 lists a myriad of writing activities across content areas that can be chosen to challenge learners within all ability levels.

A Golden Opportunity

Each teacher has a golden opportunity to model, teach, and make writing assignments fulfilling experiences for his students. Textbooks and materials provide excellent facts and concepts to involve and challenge the young author. The activities expose students to the different genres, styles, and types of writing in the real world. The students grow in their ability to write with each experience in and out of the classroom. The teacher's passion for the subject is instilled in students through intriguing hooks, modeling, and meaningful writing activities. One teacher's interest can excite a learner and build confidence in his writing ability. One stimulating assignment may motivate a student to become a fluent author.

The Authors' Hope

The strategies and activities in this resource were created by the authors or adapted from effective practices. Many lists, definitions, and activities are designed for the student to use. Words of encouragement, tips, and practical applications are included. Each strategy may be used as a writing tool to enhance thinking and learning in differentiated

Figure 0.2 Writing Across the Content Areas

Subject	Language Arts	Social Studies	Math	Science	Visual Arts	Vocational Studies	Physical Education and Health
Uses of Writing	Journals	Data gathering	Data interpretation	Data	Journals	Lists	Rules
	Diaries	Research	Summaries	Charts	Critiques	Directions	Notes
	Critiques	Notes	Conclusions	Graphs	Summaries	Inventions	Posters
	Summaries	Interviews	Word problems	Interviews	Explanations	Interpretations	Brochures
	Procedures	Graphs	Procedures	Songs	Directions	Explanations	Captions
	Class notes	Map labels	Timelines	Experiments	Playbills	Procedures	Cheers
	Brainstorming	Statistics	Charts	Notes	Songs	Instructions	Instructions
	Manuals	Timelines	Class notes	Observations	Poems	Portfolios	Diagrams
	Ads	Reports	Labels	Logs	Interpretations	Opinions	Charts
	Research	Labels	Graphs	Reports	Research	Manuals	Signs
	Note cards	Charts	Diagrams	Definitions	Manuals	Labels	Plays
	Outlines	Notes	Directions	Statistics	Diaries	Reports	Outlines
	Final reports	Descriptions	Definitions	Opinions	Logs	Summaries	Tips
	Interviews	Diaries	Reports	Hypotheses	Materials	Conclusions	Definitions
	Analysis	Poems	Journals	Theories	Lists	Notes	Guides
	Opinions	Songs	Research	Captions	Plays	Captions	Handbooks
	Songs	Ads	Conclusions	E-mails	Invitations	E-mails	Biographies
	Jingles	Historical records	Rules	Summaries	Editorials	Charts	Plans
	Cheers	References	Formulas	Editorials	Conclusions	Recipes	Analyses
	Raps		Guidelines	Poems	E-mails	Interviews	Diagnosis
	Comparisons			Lists	Designs	Designs	Applications

Subject	Language Arts	Social Studies	Math	Science	Visual Arts	Vocational Studies	Physical Education and Health
Uses of Writing	Charts Graphs Poems Interpretations Statistics Observations Notes Reflections Editorials Letters E-mails News flashes	Lists Logs E-mails Brainstorming History Reflections Graphic organizers	Progress report Self-evaluation Statistics Comparisons Brainstorming Analyses Reflections Notes	Labels Research Inventions Graphic organizers Problem Procedure Diagnosis	Creations Inventions Charts Graphic organizers Signs Notes Articles Portfolio Captions	Brainstorming Rules Charts Lists Reflections Evaluate	Agreements Contracts Game reviews Medical advice Player biographies Newspaper articles First-aid directions Promotions Game statistics

classrooms. We hope the ideas presented are adapted to teach information in all curriculum areas to develop successful, confident, enthusiastic writers.

Our Mission

Our mission is twofold: (1) To teach students how to use writing as an effective learning tool and (2) to encourage and assist all teachers as they use writing as a valuable component of instruction in the differentiated classrooms. Educators often target skills for writing improvement in daily lessons and test preparations. However, we seldom see a student's self-satisfaction, enjoyment, empowerment, or confidence considered in formal plans to improve writing skills. Writers must know the purpose for each skill, strategy, or experience. They must find the activity to be appealing, so they will have a desire to complete the task.

Refer to each writer as an author. The title will increase the learner's confidence. Throughout this guide, writers are referred to as authors. Each learner must believe in his writing ability and know that he is an author. He needs assurance that each writing attempt is respected and appreciated.

Creating a 1
Climate for
Writing

When a butterfly egg is hatched in a proper environment,
It has everything needed to thrive.
When a child enters the writing world,
He has everything he needs to become an effective author.

In a differentiated classroom, the climate is conducive to writing. It is a comfortable, exciting place for any student author. All aspects of the physical and psychological environment have been established with the students' individual needs in mind. Lessons include activities that motivate and challenge the young authors. Novel writing strategies, materials, and tools are used to intrigue the writers.

The young authors feel secure in taking risks with their ideas and skills during writing exercises. They view their mistakes as opportunities to improve. They know errors are corrected with specific, positive feedback and encouragement. The teacher schedules ample time for the writers to complete assignments at their own pace.

The students understand the value of writing to learn and communicate ideas. The teacher guides young authors to see the value of expressing emotions and thoughts in their unique styles. Writing experiences provide opportunities for the students to see themselves as authors. The students develop a deep appreciation for published authors through exposure to a variety of genres. The teacher shares the joy of writing daily.

CREATE AN ENVIRONMENT THAT MOTIVATES THE WRITER

Instill Self-Efficacy

Self-efficacy creates the "I Believe in Me!" feeling. It is an individual's belief in his ability. Self-efficacy has a great influence on an individual's decision about the activities he chooses, the amount of effort he will expend, and his level of achievement related to learning (Zimmerman, Bandura, & Martinez-Pons, 1992). The student must believe his writing ability is developed through successful writing experiences.

The writer's self-efficacy is cultivated and instilled when positive comments provide recommendations for improvement. Each writing experience develops the student's self-efficacy or belief that he is a successful author. The writer's self-doubt or "I can't" feeling must be replaced with self-confidence, the "I can" feeling.

Develop Self-Regulated Learners

Self-regulated students monitor and control their thought processes in order to learn. Zimmerman, Bonner, and Kovach (1996) presented the following model that may be used to plan self-regulated learning experiences for writers: (1) self-evaluation and monitoring, (2) goal setting and strategic planning, (3) putting a plan into action and monitoring it, and (4) monitoring outcomes and refining strategies. Students need to know how to think about their thinking as self-regulated learners.

Personal self-monitoring of one's thoughts is referred to as *metacognition*. Metacognitive activity takes place when a student uses purposeful thinking strategies (Ferrari & Sternberg, 1998). Teachers must guide students through the thinking processes that accompany writing experiences before, during, and after each activity. The student's thought processes are spoken, so the teacher can monitor them. When the learner demonstrates a thorough understanding and ability to mentally apply the strategy correctly and automatically, the teacher guides him to apply the skills silently. This self-talk leads a self-regulated learner through the thinking needed to complete tasks. For example, when several writing topics are presented as choices, students use self-talk to review their knowledge on the various subjects so they can select the most familiar theme. During a writing activity, students know to ask themselves periodically if the sentences are in sequential order and support the main idea. After writing, the students know to follow a checklist to see that everything is complete. They need time to apply and process the new material.

Opportunities to work independently foster self-regulated learning. When groups have assignments, each student is responsible for various aspects of the final report or presentation.

Young authors must know and understand the thinking processes that accompany writing skills and strategies. Teachers inspire self-regulated learning by modeling, personalizing learning experiences, and exhibiting high expectations.

Develop Internal Motivation

The learner's enthusiasm, effort, and energy used in accomplishing a task or participating in an activity are driven by his or her internal motivation. Some factors involved in intrinsic motivation include self-determination, curiosity, challenge, and effort (Santrock, 2001). The writer's internal goals are determined by his motivation or desire to achieve. Teachers nurture this desire to participate and to accomplish tasks.

A student's motivation increases when he is given choices and responsibility for learning (Stipek, 1996). Two of the strongest motivators are interest and curiosity (Lipsitz, 1984).

The teacher's excitement for learning subject matter is contagious. Intrinsic motivation is a key factor in developing a self-motivated, self-directed writer.

The student's desire to associate with others or to work alone should be considered in each lesson design. Strategically plan flexible groupings to include time for total group, independent, partner, and small group writing activities. Create a team spirit to fulfill the learner's need to belong to a group. Encourage the student to set personal learning goals for improvement. When students become self-directed or self-motivated, optimal learning occurs. Teachers must fuel the learners' motivation to generate and maintain their internal drive and zest for writing.

CREATE A SAFE AND POSITIVE WRITING ATMOSPHERE

In a safe writing environment, the authors' work is accepted. They know that each piece of writing is special and is treated with respect. In this atmosphere, the students are eager to participate in writing experiences. The teacher creates a personalized environment that motivates, challenges, and stimulates the authors' desire to write.

If a student has a red mark phobia because his errors have been emphasized, he is likely to avoid writing, even if he knows the content information. In a safe environment, each mistake is viewed as an opportunity to improve. The student needs time to correct individual work, to make improvements needed, and to share writing accomplishments.

The environment is nonthreatening, so students feel free to take risks. The students have opportunities to express themselves in an atmosphere of open communication. Students who think "out of the box" are praised.

Displayed sayings, charts, and other visuals reflect the teacher's positive expectations.

Slogans and Poster Ideas

- Write, Write, Write!
- We are authors. We write!
- We talk! We write! We share!
- If I can say it, I can write it!
- The more I write the better author I will be!

The Four B's for Writing (A Poster Sample)

Be there.   Pretend you are in the scene.

Be brief.   Make words count. If you are too wordy, the message will be buried.

Be clear.   Express your thoughts with words everyone will understand.

Be positive.   Write your message in positive terms, especially when the context is negative.

In a safe environment, the uniqueness of each individual's writing is emphasized. The writing may be difficult to read. It may contain some incorrect word usage and mechanics, but it will be the author's writing. Teach the student to take pride in each writing experience. Build self-efficacy or confidence by giving the student ownership of his writing. One way to accomplish this task is to ask the student to read his work orally and sign each piece as the author! For example, the writer signs, "Author, Susan Jones."

CREATE AN EXCITING WRITING ENVIRONMENT

Razzmatazz to Thingamajigs

Provide an exciting writing environment, so the student looks forward to the activities. Build anticipation into the experiences, so the learner will be eager to work with new topics. Use "unknowns" to intrigue and stimulate curiosity. Constantly entice the student with unique writing materials and instruments.

Use materials related to the content to build interest and motivate the writer. Match the materials to the assignment. For example, if the student is studying Japan, use rice paper. If he is learning about the Bill of Rights, use parchment paper. If he is involved in an oceanography unit, use sand.

Cool Tools

Vary the size, color, shape, and texture of writing implements. A student may write better with larger or smaller tools. He may write better with an ink pen or a pencil. The following list provides suggestions for novel writing implements and materials. Add more instruments to the list to enhance content writing experiences.

TRY THESE COOL TOOLS

Brushes	Chalk	Chocolate	Clay	Crayons
Dough	Glitter	Glue	Icing	Markers
Paint	Pebbles	Strings	Thread	Sand

Pens (colored, felt, gel, glitter, calligraphy, ink, or quill)
Pencils (fat, skinny, colored, or lead)

Material Magic

Most writing assignments in schools are completed on notebook paper with a pencil. Spice up activities by varying the media, the size, shape, color, weight, and texture of the writing materials. Correlate the materials with the topic of study. The use of variety in writing materials will keep students tuned in to the topics and hook them on assignments.

Anticipation is an effective motivator. Generate curiosity with a variety of Material Magic. Use the following materials to capture the authors' attention and ham up the teaching act:

TRY SOME MATERIAL MAGIC

Construction paper	Chalkboard	Charts	Parchment paper
Dry erase boards	Wallpaper	Fabric	Cards
Cardboard	Designed paper		

Note: Ask a local print shop to save different types, sizes, textures, and colors of scrap paper. Newspaper offices often donate "end rolls" of newsprint. This provides the class with a variety of free paper for writing experiences.

Make the Size Fit

It is fun to fit the writing assignments to various paper sizes. To choose the paper size needed, think about how much space the student needs to answer the question. For example, if the response calls for a small bit of information, use a small piece of paper. Try a long skinny piece of paper for a list of information. Use a large piece of paper for group activities, so everyone can work together and see the writing. Often the paper size helps answer that old, familiar question, "How much do we have to write?"

The Shape of Things

Use a shape that directly correlates with the unit topic as a novel learning tool. The student will link the information written with the shape. For example, use a banner to display a logo, slogan, or goal to emphasize information. Record nature information on material shaped like a leaf, flower, or tree. Graphic organizers are popular learning tools. They may be designed in various shapes. For example, use an octopus shape to record facts learned in an oceanography unit. Use a rocket with a space study.

Rainbow Casting

Color stimulates the mind and evokes thoughts and feelings. Use colors to correlate with the topic. Provide color choices to bring out the student's best writing.

EXAMPLES

- Record a historical battle on gray paper.
- Reflect on new learning using green to represent growth.

Ready References

Make various reference sources available, so students will have free access to them. Update and replenish the materials as the topics change. Ask the students for suggestions to add to the resource collection. The sources may include the following:

Teacher notes	Directions	Pictures	Word banks	Books	Dictionaries
Encyclopedias	Timelines	Charts	References	Graphs	Thesauruses
Maps	Magazines	Computer software			

FIND THE RIGHT SPOT FOR THE WRITE SPOT!

Would an adult write letters or grocery lists at a formal dining room table? If he is like most people, he grabs a snack with something to drink and finds a comfortable place to write. When the individual tires from sitting too long or experiences writer's block, he moves. He may engage in another task, go for a walk, or simply relax. Often thoughts for the writing task start floating around in his mind while he is relaxing. After the break, he returns to his writing with new ideas. This is what authors do!

Why are writing experiences at home so different from those at school? Do the experiences have to be different? No. In classrooms, authors need seating choices. Some may spend hours seated at the computer composing documents. Others may choose a place to lie down in a comfortable place with a laptop or a writing pad. After a long time period, this comfortable spot often becomes very uncomfortable. The physical need for a change becomes the student's priority. A break or change in position may refocus his mind and enhance his flow of ideas.

Create writing areas that correlate with units of study. For example, use a teepee during a study of Native Americans or a table turned upside down to represent the boat George Washington used in his famous crossing of the Delaware. Write Spots may contain sleeping bags, pillows from home, couches, or stuffed animals. A comfortable corner may have a special pillow, a reading lamp, a beanbag chair, or a soft rug. The student benefits from opportunities to choose or create a comfortable Write Spot. Of course, the teacher has the final approval.

Suggestions for Designing the Write Spot

- Designate and label a special, comfortable, and appealing area for writing.
- Post directions, rules, or guidelines as expectations.
- Provide various paper sizes, colors, textures, and shapes.
- Use a variety of unique implements to stimulate interest.
- Provide word lists.
- Supply reference books and materials.
- Provide art supplies such as scissors and glue for creative activities.
- Make computers with word processing programs available.
- Give choices.
- Provide display spaces with directions for mounting the work.
- Create cozy areas with pillows, comfortable chairs, couches, and rugs.
- Use writing lamps.
- Play background music for added relaxation.

Sensational Centers

Designate special areas of the room as writing nooks, centers, or stations. The centers can be used for specific assignments or for exploration. The work completed in the center should have an academic focus and purpose to connect it to the content information. A writing center must be a place for productive learning. If the student is wasting time at the center, add relevant or high-interest activities. It may be necessary to post a sign over the center that states, "Closed Until Further Notice!" Sensational Centers provide a place for the student to work on writing assignments alone, with a partner, or with a small group. Enhance learning and creativity with Cool Tools and Material Magic in the sensational writing center.

ESTABLISH AUTHOR OWNERSHIP

Be Aware of Feelings and Emotions

Be aware of the student's feelings as he or she approaches writing assignments. If a student does not feel he can write or does not like to write, the insecurity will hamper his performance. Attitudes play a major role in writing success. Plan opportunities for the student who has little confidence in his writing ability. This student needs to write on familiar topics. Identify and remove emotional barriers to promote self-expression and develop successful authors. (See the attitude surveys in Chapter 2.)

Provide Choices

When a student is allowed to choose his own goal, he is more likely to be motivated to work and accomplish it (Schunk, 1996). Choices provide the student with feelings of ownership and a deeper sense of personal responsibility and pride in his work.

Standards are required, but choices can bring desired results. The writer's product must fit the goal or assessment tool when choices are offered. All activities and directions may be assigned. Somewhere in the writing process, however, students need opportunities to make decisions. Teachers should be aware of the writing experiences that are presented as choices. This establishes the author's ownership and independence as a writer.

ASSESS THE WRITING CLIMATE

Teachers set the tone and control the climate that influence the students' feelings and emotions during writing periods. The following list may be used to identify strengths and weaknesses in order to make a classroom or school an inviting place for writing experiences.

Place an X on the appropriate place on the line that describes the writing climate.

	Most of the Time	Rarely Ever
1. I provide a psychologically safe environment so students feel free to express ideas.		
2. I think of my classroom from the student's point of view.		
3. I model and share my writing experiences.		
4. I respect writing time and avoid interruptions.		
5. I use a variety of writing tools and materials.		
6. I emphasize the value of daily improvements more than grades.		
7. I use specific praise to correct writing.		
8. I encourage writing through my verbal and nonverbal behaviors.		
9. I use open-ended questions to encourage divergent responses.		
10. I vary genres in writing assignments.		
11. I give encouragement to the struggling author.		
12. I provide exciting writing opportunities within units of study.		
13. I use constructive criticism when improvements are needed.		
14. The student is given opportunities to share in various ways.		
15. I provide ample time for writing with content information.		
16. It is obvious to each student that I am excited about writing activities.		

My improvement goal is _____.
I can improve the writing environment by _____.

In differentiated classrooms, the teachers encourage the young authors to use their talents, interests, and personality in their writing. The students discover the joy of writing through enjoyable experiences.

A positive, stimulating writing climate motivates writers to become authors for a lifetime. Each student knows "this is the way we do things around here" (Gregory & Chapman, 2001, p. 8). It is up to the teacher to establish this learning culture for a community of inspired writers.

Knowing 2
the Writer

*A butterfly evolves through developmental stages to
become a beautiful, winged creature.
A student evolves through stages to become an
effective writer and author.*

STAGES OF A WRITER

Teachers observe authors as they evolve through developmental writing
stages. Individual students may go through all stages, or they may skip a
stage. The stages are identified in activities such as journal writing or other
first-draft writing opportunities.

When a child makes his first marks with a crayon, pencil, or marker, he
is experimenting with the writer's craft and mimicking adults around him.
He evolves through the developmental stages if he is engaged in appropriate writing experiences. During each stage, he needs opportunities to
practice and experiment and receive support and praise. His writing
expertise develops from the young scribbler to the distinguished author
throughout his life.

Students need acceptance as writers and acknowledgment as authors.
The student authors should read their own writing. If corrections for errors
are nonthreatening, the students are more likely to become fluent writers.
The developmental writing stages are presented here with descriptions,
characteristics, and teaching suggestions for younger and older students.
In every differentiated classroom, the teacher recognizes and honors the
diverse stages of writers.

Scribbler

Scribblers make bold marks haphazardly on their papers to write their stories. These marks, with straight and curving lines, are the first signs of writing. The marks express the student's feelings and ideas. He imitates writing modeled by his parents, siblings, teachers, friends, and other individuals in his world. During the scribbling experiences, the child's muscles are developing to hold the writing implement, eye-hand coordination is strengthening, and attitudes toward writing are forming.

Sometimes a scribbler identifies and describes his marks. For example, a child may scribble with various colors and say, "This is my car." Accept and praise the child's drawing so he will tell a story about his marks.

The Younger Student

As children enter the world of writing, they need crayons, markers, and pencils to develop the fine motor skills they will use when formal writing begins. The young author needs to have experiences with Cool Tools before his first school experience, so he will be ready to write. A child must know the rules for experimenting with writing. Establish the proper places to write, such as on paper, a chalkboard, or a dry erase board. Praise all marks made in appropriate places. Children who have had no writing experiences before school need opportunities to develop their fine motor skills and their writing interests after they enter the classroom.

The Older Student

An older student may be in the first developmental writing stages. This student does not enjoy writing because he fears failure. A student who is learning the English language is in this stage. He uses letter symbols to write in the new language. Instead of scribbles, the writing includes words from his native language.

Picture Maker

The Picture Maker draws a simple picture and tells a detailed story. Letters or numbers may appear anywhere in the drawing.

The Younger Student

The Picture Maker draws as a form of writing. He does not have to know letters of the alphabet or the appropriate combinations of the letters to form the words. He draws pictures to express his thoughts instead of writing words. Often the pictures are unrecognizable to adults. The child knows each detail in his picture and can tell a story about it. To encourage elaboration and details, ask the child questions that lead him to tell more about the drawing.

- Tell me about your picture.
- What can you add to your picture?
- Wow! Tell me about it.

An effective activity to use with a student at this stage is to fold a piece of paper in half. The student draws a picture on the top section with his crayons. Instruct the student to put his crayons away and turn his paper to the bottom half. Give him time to write his story with his pencil on the bottom half of the paper. Tell him to open his paper so he views his paper and his writing as he reads his story aloud to a partner or the teacher. The teacher has the option to create a Language Experience as the child tells his story. If this option is chosen, the teacher says, "I am going to write the words you say as you tell me about your picture." As the child relates his story, the teacher writes his words on the bottom half of the paper. The student sees his thoughts become words on the paper. This models writing. The student follows each word as the teacher reads and writes the story. During this experience, the child builds the concept that the picture and the words tell the story.

The Older Student

An older student who finds it difficult to write his thoughts may be able to record his ideas in picture form. This student is visual in his thinking and sees the pictures in his head. If given the opportunity to see the thoughts in his mind, and draw a picture before he writes, he creates a more complete story. Question the student about his visual images to help him see the picture in his mind more clearly. When he adds details to his picture, more details will appear in his writing. Remember, a Picture Maker works well with graphic organizers. Teach this student to think it, see it, and draw it before he writes it.

Storyteller

A Storyteller tells the story well. He writes familiar letters and numbers he knows. He writes them randomly in a scribble form. This learner mimics the writers he observes.

The Younger Student

Allow time for the Storyteller to write, even though an observer cannot always read the message. As the student reads and tells the story, write the story to model writing for him. This continues the practice of writing the young author's story as it was demonstrated in the Picture Maker stage. Another way to meet the Storyteller's needs is to provide the time and place for him to record his story on a cassette, listen to it, and then write it. Remind him to write the words exactly as he hears them.

The Older Student

An older student who is a Storyteller tells the story or answers an open-ended question orally, but he cannot get his words down on paper. He needs someone to write the story so he sees his words written through the modeling.

The Storyteller and Invented Spelling

Encourage the Storyteller to use invented spelling, so he gives more details and continues to elaborate. When this student must concentrate on spelling, he becomes frustrated and loses interest in creating the story. Invented spelling encourages him to use words that are difficult to spell. If conventional spelling rules are enforced, this student often chooses easy words that he knows how to spell. The acceptance of invented spelling fosters creativity and higher-order thinking skills because the writer focuses on the content and organization of his thoughts.

Letter Shaker

The Letter Shaker draws a picture and labels it with random letters placed all over the drawing. The reader occasionally recognizes a familiar word.

The Younger Student

The younger Letter Shaker relates to the written symbols in his environment. He does not know the difference between letters and words. He understands the connections between the letters and their sounds. The Letter Shaker points to a letter and says a word when he tells his story. This appears when the teacher is introducing the letters and their sounds. After the child writes his story, the teacher writes the story as the child tells it. When a letter or word is recognized in the Letter Shaker's writing, the teacher draws a line from the letter or word in the story to the student's representation for the word. The child needs praise for using correct letters or words.

Copier

The Copier writes words around him to pretend he is writing a story. In this stage, the child has linked phrases and sentences to the act of writing.

The Younger Student

The Copier uses words or sentences in the room in his writing. He uses the words or sentences to pretend that he is a writer. For example, he may copy, "Fall is here," from a bulletin board. He looks at these words and tells his own unrelated, personal story. He tells a story while looking at the writing. The author is the only one who can read the work. He realizes that words in the environment may be used in his writing.

As the Copier develops, he needs a print-rich environment with vocabulary words displayed. For example, use word walls, posters, and labeled objects. He needs access to resources such as dictionaries and pictionaries. Students in this stage benefit from using a rebus, since it is a picture labeled with the word.

The Older Student

The older student copies printed material from various resources and claims it as his writing. He knows he must get words down on his paper. Often he does not comprehend what he has written. He may not have the confidence to put the information in his own words. He needs to learn step-by-step writing procedures such as plagiarism laws and note taking.

Sound Maker

The Sound Maker understands the letter-and-sound connection. This is obvious when he writes important parts of words the way they sound.

The Younger Student

The younger Sound Maker writes the sounds he hears in a word. Usually these letters represent sounds at the beginning or the end of the words. He is able to read the words aloud. This is the initial stage of invented spelling. Usually the student no longer creates long stories to tell. He strategically reads the words represented with letters. This is a beginning stage for the student to become an accurate reader of his own work.

A picture guides the Sound Maker to stay on the main idea. When he reads the story, he says the words represented by the letters. Allow him to point to the letters, so he makes the reading and writing connection. Write the Sound Maker's story for him. Draw a line from the letter in the word to the letter the student wrote. Give the student praise for using a letter in the word. For example, the student says, "I have a ball," and then writes the letters, "ihab." The teacher draws a line from each letter to the word it represents in the sentence. Stories may be short because the student concentrates on letter sounds.

The Older Student

The older student using invented spelling is a Letter Shaker on a higher level. This student knows the letter sounds or some letters in the word. When he comes to a word he does not know how to spell, he writes the letters he hears or remembers. Invented spelling allows an author to write without interrupting the flow of his thoughts.

Sentence Maker

The Sentence Maker writes sentences about the topic and uses invented spelling. Usually these sentences relate to the main idea. He understands that his words create thoughts and tell a story. This applies to the *younger* or *older student* in his writing world. Skills and tools of mechanics used correctly in sentences are mastered. For example, when a student uses the correct punctuation mark at the end of a sentence, he has mastered that skill. This skill is a part of the student's knowledge base for future lessons on punctuation.

Story Maker

A Story Maker organizes the content of his story with a beginning, middle, and ending. He uses style in his writing. He knows how to write complete sentences. Main ideas and supporting details are evident. The author runs some letters together and spaces other letters correctly. He automatically applies the mastered skills and mechanics of writing. For example, he spells a word correctly if he has learned how to spell it. The Story Maker stage is found in the writing of *younger* and *older students*. A Story Maker yearns to share his work because writing has become a rewarding, pleasant experience. He needs praise and honor as an author. Celebrate his growth as a writer.

WRITING AND THE BRAIN

Make Mental Connections

According to David Sousa (2001), "Teachers try to change the human brain every day. The more they know about how it learns, the more successful they can be" (p. 3). The latest brain research provides information about the best approaches to engage the student's mind for optimal learning. For instance, the brain pays attention to meaningful information. When writing skills and strategies are presented in ways that link the prior information to the new information and the student's practical world, he is more likely to remember and use it.

If the student has had prior experiences with a topic, mental pictures and feelings are activated when the topic is mentioned. Consider the student's prior writing experiences, so new skills and strategies can be based on the learner's experiences and level of understanding. (See Adjustable Assignments in Chapters 4 and 5.)

Build Long-Term Memory

A student's ability to remember new information depends on his previous knowledge (Keil, 1999). Teachers plan new writing concepts and knowledge to make connections with the student's prior knowledge. New information is reconstructed to fit the learner's schema as it is stored in memory.

The writer needs to think about the best way to store the information he is learning. The term *metamemory* was coined by Chapman and King (2000) to emphasize the importance of teaching a student various ways to think about the memory strategy he is using.

> If I see the purpose,
> If I understand it,
> If I know how to use it,
> If I need it,
> I will remember it and use it.
>
> —Chapman & King, 2003

Flow

Csikszentmihalyi (1990) studied motivation and described optimal learning experiences as a state of flow. *Flow* is a state of mind that occurs when the student is totally immersed in a writing activity. When he is in this state, he concentrates on the task at hand while experiencing happiness and joy. In this state, the learner is not easily distracted. The state of flow is observed when individuals are engaged in a favorite writing activity of interest. The desire to be involved is obvious. This intrinsic motivation occurs when the student is challenged with successful writing experiences. Flow does not occur when the learner is bored or frustrated.

LEARNING STYLES AND MULTIPLE INTELLIGENCES

An individual's learning style is his preferred way to use his abilities. Each student has many preferences for learning. The most common learning style models include (1) auditory, (2) visual, (3) kinesthetic, and (4) tactile or hands-on learning. When learning styles are used in planning, one student may learn the steps in the writing process by creating a rap with a partner. Another student may prefer to work alone and design a graphic organizer to learn the steps.

Gardner's Multiple Intelligences Theory

The Multiple Intelligence Theory was developed by Dr. Howard Gardner when he was studying how the brain works. This theory proved that every brain is unique with areas of weaknesses and strengths. Weak areas can be strengthened. Everyone becomes more intelligent through their personal experiences, interests, and life's opportunities. Teachers use Dr. Gardner's eight intelligences to label the intelligence targets in lesson planning; for example, designing a collage is a visual assignment. This labels the activity or strategy to be taught, not the students. Students have enough labels (Chapman, 1993).

The multiple intelligences identified by Gardner are

1. **Verbal/Linguistic:** Using language for communication with reading, writing, listening, speaking, and linking information

2. **Musical/Rhythmic:** Being sensitive to and using rhythm, beat, pitch, tone, timbre, and inflection

3. **Logical/Mathematical:** Solving problems and abstract thinking; using the number and pattern world

4. **Visual/Spatial:** Exploring art and all media, working with colors, visualizing and interpreting spatial relationships

5. **Bodily/Kinesthetic:** Using movement, touch, tactile, and hands-on learning; the mind/body relationship

6. **Naturalist:** Adapting and surviving in one's world, studying and labeling nature; understanding and using nature in a personal way

7. **Intrapersonal:** Working alone, setting goals; self-directed, personalized, or independent learning

8. **Interpersonal:** Working with others, socializing, empathizing, and cooperating

Genetically, each person is born with a unique brain. Through experiences, an individual becomes more intelligent throughout his life. He grows more intelligent through experiences, opportunities, exposure, and interests. Everyone has areas of weakness that can be strengthened. This is the reason information may be important to the teacher but may not be important to the learner.

This theory impacts instruction because teachers teach in their strongest intelligence areas. Everyone has three to four strong areas. When teachers use their weaker intelligence areas to teach, they are working in areas of discomfort. A teacher will do whatever is necessary to reach a student, so he may find it necessary to teach in his discomfort zones when these areas may be the student's strong areas.

Sternberg's Triarchy Theory

Dr. Robert Sternberg's studies involve the brain and how it works. His Triarchy Theory of intelligence involves practical, analytical, and creative thinking processes. He believes each individual learns using these three ways of learning, but some individuals have a dominant area. For example, the student who is an analytical learner usually excels in traditional academic programs. Sternberg's theory may be used to understand how a writer approaches a task or a challenge.

WRITERS WRITING IN THE CONTENT AREAS

Writers Write to Demonstrate Understanding

Teachers use writing assignments in content areas because they provide easy, quick assessments of a student's knowledge. There is not enough time to listen to each student's oral responses. Writing is one of the most efficient ways to check individual understanding of specific topics.

Writers Write to Enhance Learning and Memory

Writing is a tool for learning. When a student writes about a topic, his understanding is enhanced (Benton, 1997). The author identifies the information stored in his memory and organizes it, so his readers or listeners understand it. This mental processing provides the author with opportunities to think about the information as his ideas form and to think about it again as the actual writing is completed.

Writing activates memory as information enters the learner's schema and mental pathways. For information to enter long-term memory, the student must connect prior experiences and current information to build new learning. Writing activities create these bridges, making it easier for learners to recall information for academic activities, daily use, and tests.

Writers Write to Inform and to Express
Important Ideas in the Real World

To make his writing experiences meaningful, the student must understand the value of writing. He needs to see the many ways to use writing in his immediate world and the role it will have in his future. Writers in the real world write to inform, to learn, and to express ideas. Teachers can discuss the many reasons individuals write before assigning the activities that follow.

WRITERS WRITE TO

- Analyze and solve problems
- Express feelings including anger, joy, laughter, or sadness
- Share secrets, personal ideas, and interests
- Share experiences, wildest ideas, and discoveries
- Record information
- Share thoughts with other individuals
- Appreciate the beauty and magic of language
- Remember information for later use or study
- Become a published author
- Play with words, thoughts, and ideas
- Relax and enjoy self-expression
- Brainstorm and journal
- _____

Activities That Reinforce the Value of Writing

The following activities will help the learner realize the value of knowing how to write.

Activity: Here, There, Everywhere

1. Brainstorm the many ways writing is used in and out of the school.

2. Record responses on a chart.

3. Challenge the student to add to the chart throughout the year as he discovers new ways writing is used in his life.

EXAMPLES

Advertisements	Books	Menus	Charts
Newspapers	Notes	Signs	Labels

Activity: A View Through Interview

Tell the student to choose a person to interview about the use of writing in that person's career and daily life. Include heroes, experts in a field, leaders, cooks, salespeople, and politicians. Ask the student to formulate questions before the interviews take place. Use interview questions similar to the examples presented here:

1. How do you use writing in your work?

2. How do you use writing at home?

3. Do you like to write?

4. Do you use e-mail? How?

5. How does writing help you?

6. Could you work without writing?

Activity: Writing in the World of Work

Figure 2.1 can be used with the following activity to make students aware of the formal and informal uses of writing.

1. Form four sets of partners.

2. Assign each career in the center box to a partner team.

3. One member of the partner team is assigned the informal side of writing in the career. The other partner is responsible for the formal aspects of writing.

4. The partner members work together to brainstorm and record the informal and formal ways writing is used in the career assigned.

5. Each partner uses the brainstormed information to compose an article or report about the uses of writing in the career.

Figure 2.1   Writing in the World of Work

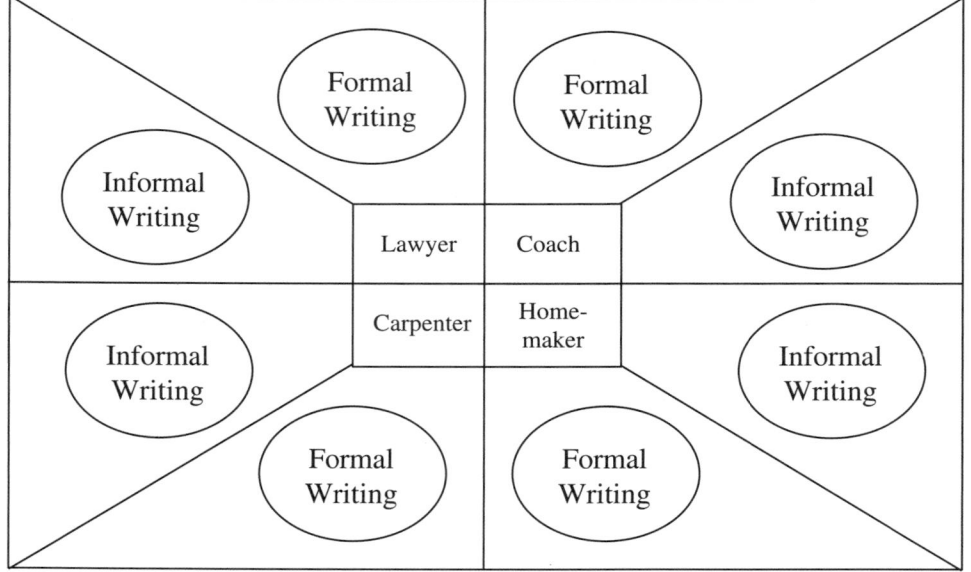

Diagnosing and Assessing Writers 3

Varied designs and colors make each butterfly unique.
Varied interests, styles, and skills make each writer unique.

KNOWING THE AUTHORS

Teachers in the content areas who assign writing tasks are often the first to observe student writing problems. Following are descriptions of the sorts of behaviors teachers are likely to encounter in the differentiated classroom when students are asked to write. The diagnosis and prescription sections of this chapter contain suggestions to assist the teacher in solving each student's writing problems. With appropriate guidance, students can usually overcome obstacles that stand in their way and become fluent writers.

Drawing Dana

OBSERVABLE BEHAVIOR

- Enjoys drawing
- Shows what she knows in pictures
- Replaces a word or phrases with a drawing
- Draws when given a choice
- Is a doodler

Feelings of the Student

- I like to draw. If I draw first, I write better.
- I would rather draw than write.
- Drawing helps me understand information.
- I like to work with a partner or a small group so I can draw the poster.

Suggested Prescriptions

- Permit drawing as a prewriting activity.
- Allow the author to illustrate her writing.
- Teach and encourage her to create graphic organizers to plot information and organize thinking.

Insecure Inez

Observable Behaviors

- Does not believe she can write
- Lacks confidence
- Has the ability to write, but becomes easily frustrated
- Is shy about sharing own work

Feelings of the Student

- I'm afraid I will fail.
- I want to please everyone.
- I remember my last writing assignment had many red marks all over it.
- I cannot write like my friends.
- My writing always embarrasses me.

Suggested Prescriptions

- Give shorter assignments.
- Use specific praise and encouragement.
- Assign topics that target her favorite subjects.
- Assign an empathetic partner.
- Plan successful experiences.

Lollygagging Lonnie

Observable Behaviors

- Slow to finish
- Wastes time
- Swayed off task easily
- Lacks confidence

FEELINGS OF THE STUDENT

- I don't want to be the last one to finish.
- Everyone always tells me to "hurry up" or "stop wasting time."
- I would rather do anything else than write.
- I wish teachers would let me write about a subject that I know.
- I am interested in many things but not this assignment.
- I don't want to write about this topic because I don't know very much about it.

SUGGESTED PRESCRIPTIONS

- Begin with brief assignments.
- Use a timer.
- Allow choices for personal places to write.
- Select high-interest topics.
- Use story starters or prompts.

Stumped Stan

OBSERVABLE BEHAVIORS

- Stops to spell correctly
- Experiences writer's block and says, "I can't think of anything to write"
- Shows fear of failure; says, "I do not like this"
- Waits for help
- Gets off task often
- Exhibits learned helplessness created by depending on the thinking of the teacher, classmates, parents, or other adults

FEELINGS OF THE STUDENT

- I don't know how to spell this word, and I can't write any more until I find out.
- I can't think of what to write for this next part.
- I just looked at that last night, and now I can't remember it.
- I feel frustrated. I wish I could write like all of my friends.
- I'm afraid I will be wrong.
- I get so embarrassed during writing time.

SUGGESTED PRESCRIPTIONS

- Build confidence with specific, positive feedback.
- Provide guided practice.
- Plan strategically for successful experiences.
- Explain the purpose of the first draft.

- Develop knowledge and experiences with the topic prior to writing assignments.
- Use prompts, including pictures.
- Implement effective prewriting activities to collect thoughts and organize information.
- Allow extra time to complete work.

Wordy Wilma

OBSERVABLE BEHAVIORS

- Is redundant
- Uses run-on sentences
- Rambles, goes on and on
- Tries to use "big" words
- Repeats thoughts in several ways

FEELINGS OF THE STUDENT

- I can tell that people do not like the way I express my thoughts.
- I have to give all the details so people listening to me will understand.
- When I meet with my teacher, a friend, or a small group to revise my paper, they always make a lot of corrections.
- I am not a good writer.

SUGGESTED PRESCRIPTIONS

- Model quality writing.
- Use an organizer to gather and outline thoughts.
- Draw lines through unnecessary words, phrases, and sentences in the first draft.
- Provide an effective prewriting activity.
- Record her story orally and ask her to write the exact words she used.
- Teach her to tell the story aloud before writing it.

Author Arthur

OBSERVABLE BEHAVIORS

- Enjoys writing
- Is creative and confident
- Sees himself as an author
- Writes for pleasure

FEELINGS OF THE STUDENT

- I like to write. It is one of my favorite things to do.
- I am an author.
- I have so many ideas I want to write.
- I have favorite genres that I like to use.
- I make lists, set goals, and write e-mails and letters to my friends.
- I take notes to remember important information.

SUGGESTED PRESCRIPTIONS

- Provide positive writing opportunities.
- Encourage. Do not squelch his enthusiasm.
- Give some choices.
- Provide experiences to perfect skills.
- Honor the individual's style of writing.
- Provide publishing opportunities.

Author Arthur is the writer who has the abilities educators want to develop in all students. This author is able to create style and is successful as a writer.

WHAT IF STUDENTS REFUSE TO WRITE?

- Hook them on the topic.
- Use informal writing.
- Revise author-selected pieces.
- Provide reassurance.
- Accept invented spelling.
- Use many first drafts.
- Motivate and praise.
- Explain writing for quality, not quantity.
- Teach the value of mistakes.
- Require fewer Neat Sheets.
- Celebrate each success.
- Vary the forms of writing.
- Give opportunities for writing enjoyment in each student's areas of interest.

More Frequent Writing Problems

Have a conference with the student who has a writing problem. Ask him to describe his writing problem. Listen to his view or self-analysis. Conference privately, so the student will not be embarrassed. Ask the student to brainstorm reasons for his difficulty with the task. Listen.

Following are common writing problems and some suggested prescriptions to analyze individual writing performances.

Writing Problem	Prescriptions
Doesn't want to write	• Allow to write on his interests • Model and write with the student • Write with others
Is unfamiliar with the topic	• Provide the background needed to write • Brainstorm a list of topics for choice
Lacks prewriting skills	• Model brainstorming • Use partner or small group brainstorming • Vary strategies to record prewriting thoughts
Mumbles while writing	• Move to an area away from others • Allow to mumble, if not disturbing anyone else
Has difficulty beginning the first draft	• Accept writer's block and probe • Return to the prewriting stage • Assign choice of topics
Topic doesn't have enough depth	• Have a conversation and then show the student how to add the missing pieces • Ask probing questions • Go back to prewriting • Reread the writing thus far so student can add details • Provide more time for research
Has a physical disability	• Use a word processor • Type as the student talks • Record the oral story; write it later

Students with disabilities are not excused from assignments. They need an appropriate assignment to meet their needs. They need praise and some form of reward or compensation for initial writing efforts, followed by increased expectations with each writing success.

EFFECTIVE ASSESSMENT TOOLS

*It is physically impossible to see what is going on inside cocoons,
where the butterfly's vibrant colors and intricate designs develop.
It is physically impossible to see transformations in the author's
mind, where his writing skills and potential evolve.*

—Chapman & King 2003

Teachers can design effective checklists and rubrics for the group or individual they observe. They use these assessment tools to determine the strengths and weaknesses of a student or group of students. Teachers know the skills that need to be assessed better than anyone. Assessment provides feedback for the teacher and the learner. Teachers design assessment tools that assist the student to grow as a writer. Encourage students to be kind, critical evaluators of their peers. Train authors to use assessment tools to assess their own strengths and weaknesses.

Prepare for Assessment Scenes

Writing is a part of the formal assessment scene. Written responses to open-ended questions are required on standardized tests. The student must know how to use the basic steps of the writing process so he can organize ideas, draft, revise, and edit. When the learner knows how to recall and apply writing strategies automatically, he is able to showcase his skills. Figures 3.1, 3.2, and 3.3 illustrate suggestions, forms, and ideas to adapt for the classroom. Use the examples as needed to observe, monitor, and score writing.

Figure 3.1   Class Writing Checklist

Frequently	+
Occasionally	O
Seldom	S
Not Noted	N

Teacher _____

Class _____   Date _____

Note: List the skills to observe and assess in the writing assignment in each section. The list will vary according to the class, the skills emphasized, and the content.

Student Name	Selection Title	Skills		Comments
1.				
2.				

Figure 3.2 Essay Analysis

Student _____   Date _____

Essay Title _____

Rater: ❑ Self   ❑ Teacher   ❑ Peer   ❑ Small Group

	Yes	No	Partial	Comments
1. Selection of subject				
2. Clear content				
3. Ideas organized				
4. Message conveyed				
5. Use of details				
6. Consistent voice tense				
7. Creativity				

Figure 3.3 Individual Writing Evaluation

Name _____   Date _____

Writing Selection _____

Rater: ❑ Self   ❑ Teacher   ❑ Peer   ❑ Small Group

Writing Area	Fair	Good	Excellent	Comments
Content Contains significant information				
Organization Develops content in order				
Focus Sticks to the topic				
Mechanics Uses correct spelling and punctuation				
Other				

Rubric for Scoring Essays

A *rubric* is an evaluation tool developed with specific criteria. The criteria reflect the expectations for a product, such as a project, a report, or a presentation. The levels are used to score the writer on a particular piece of work. The levels indicate the level of assistance the student needs. Writers need to know and understand the rubric used to evaluate their work.

Student _____   Date _____

Title of Writing Selection _____

| *Scorer* |
| ☐ Self |
| ☐ Peer |
| ☐ Teacher |

5 Superior
  Used clear, descriptive sentences and paragraphs
  Organized ideas
  Included important, concise information
  Used correct mechanics
  Captured the audience's attention

4 Beyond Expectations
  Wrote with descriptive sentences
  Used correct mechanics
  Created interest for the audience

3 Acceptable
  Wrote complete sentences
  Used basic mechanics
  Held the reader's interest to some extent

2 Some Improvement Evident
  Used a few complete sentences
  Included some correct punctuation and capitalization
  Has some evidence of organization
  Low interest level shown

1 Needs Improvement
  Used incomplete sentences
  Applied incorrect punctuation and capitalization
  Beginning, middle, and end are unclear
  Work is uninteresting to the audience
  Overall Score _____

Vary terms used in rubrics to add novely to evaluations.

The following terms may be used in rubrics to set writing criteria:

Challenge students to create rubrics for their own writing evaluations.

- Great Work   Good Work   Improving   Needs Help

- Emerging   Developing   Proficient   Exemplary

- Crawling   Walking   Skipping   Running

- Tasting   Sipping   Drinking   Guzzling

Likert Scales for Scoring Writing Assignments

1. Content is on topic

   2   4   6   8
   _____

2. Organized with a flow of ideas

   2   4   6   8
   _____

3. Contains accurate information

   2   4   6   8
   _____

4. Shows author's feeling and style

   2   4   6   8
   _____

5. One of the student's "Best Works"

   2   4   6   8
   _____

The following activity will give practice in gathering information through note taking. It will give feedback to the presenter.

Scorer: ❑ Self ❑ Teacher ❑ Peer ❑ Small Group

Title of Presentation _____ Date _____

Name of Presenter _____

1. Topic presented   _____

2. Hook(s)   _____   _____

3. Supporting details   _____   _____

4. Examples provided   _____   _____

5. Value to the audience 5   4   3   2   1

6. Creativity   5   4   3   2   1

7. Closing   _____   _____

8. Strengths   _____   _____

9. Areas for improvement _____   _____

10. Content/Organization	5	4	3	2	1
Subject/Title	5	4	3	2	1
Introduction	5	4	3	2	1
Sequence	5	4	3	2	1
Details	5	4	3	2	1
Ending	5	4	3	2	1

11. Mechanics	5	4	3	2	1
Punctuation	5	4	3	2	1
Capitalization	5	4	3	2	1
Spelling	5	4	3	2	1

12. Summary comments _____

The observation checklist in Figure 3.4 is a flexible, practical tool that can be used to monitor specific skills and strategies.

Figure 3.4   Observation Checklist

Date_____   Class _____

Note: List items to be observed in the column heads.

Key: + Often   * Occasionally   → Trying

Student Names	Observable Traits					Comments
1.						
2.						

Student Surveys

The following survey examples help students understand their feelings and attitudes about themselves as writers. It is important that the students analyze and express themselves to develop confidence. This information identifies a student who needs to change negative attitudes to positive. A positive attitude is necessary for the student to develop confidence and a general interest in writing. The best surveys are developed by the teacher for an individual or specific group of students.

Revealing Feelings

1. When I am told to write, I usually feel _____. Why?

2. I am a _____writer because _____.

3. I learned to write when _____.

4. People write because they want to _____.

5. A good writer _____.

6. When others help me with my writing, I feel _____.

7. When I help others with their writing, I feel _____.

8. The worst writing assignment I have to do is _____.

9. I like to write when _____.

10. My favorite writing topics are _____.

Writer's Feelings and Performance

The following rubric is an informal assessment of a student's attitude toward writing experiences The student marks himself on the scale beside each item.

1. I enjoy writing.   Scrimmage Line --------------------- Goal Post

2. Writing is easy
   for me.   Scrimmage Line --------------------- Goal Post

3. I think and plan
   my writing.   Scrimmage Line --------------------- Goal Post

4. I revise my work
   several times.   Scrimmage Line --------------------- Goal Post

5. I read my work to
   myself.   Scrimmage Line --------------------- Goal Post

6. I enjoy reading my
   writing to a partner.   Scrimmage Line --------------------- Goal Post

7. I enjoy being an author.   Scrimmage Line --------------------- Goal Post

8. The best thing about writing is _____.

9. To be an effective writer I must have _____.

10. The worst thing about writing is _____.

11. My favorite place to write is _____.

12. When I write the answer to a discussion question, I _____
_____.

Other comments I would like to say about my feeling on writing are
_____.

Questioning the Learner

Open-Ended Questions. It is often difficult for students to respond to open-ended questions. Responses should be modeled orally before a written assignment or test is given. Ask the student to pretend he is telling answers to a friend who is listening. The "telling" will organize the information and bring better responses.

"My Open-Ended Friend"

If you see a question that has an open end,
Pretend you are telling the answer to a friend.
Write down each and every word
the way your thoughts will be heard.

> *Imagine your words flowing through your pen*
> *To answer a question with an open end.*

> —Chapman & King, 2003

Choices. Choices give a student feelings of independence and ownership for learning. Make a list of choices. For example, provide four open-ended questions for the student to answer. Ask the student to choose one question to answer.

Sixteen Words for the Wise

A student often fails to respond to open-ended writing assignments and assessments because he does not understand the terminology used in the directions. The following is a group of terms the student needs to know. Directions may be varied using these common terms in daily assignments and activities. A students needs time to discuss and apply what he is to do when the terms are used in different situations. The following explanation for open-ended key words are written in terms students can understand.

analyze	**Dig in with details.** Write obvious as well as hidden characteristics or meanings. Explain how each part functions or fits into the whole.
argue	**Give a point of view!** Take a stand and defend one side of an issue. Give facts, beliefs, opinions, and your personal view. Show your passion!
compare	**Name ways we are alike!** Comparisons provide common characteristics or attributes, identifying how things are alike or similar. Write the many ways they are the same.
contrast	**Find our differences!** Contrasts provide the characteristics or attributes that are not alike. Write how the people, events, or objects are different.
define	**Tell me!** Give meanings of the term in your own words.
demonstrate	**Show me!** Write a step-by-step procedure to show how to do something.
describe	**Let the reader see it!** Help the reader visualize and understand the object, concept, or event with your words. Use adjectives to stimulate the senses and provide attributes such as the size, shape, characteristics, color, and use. Include comparisons and contrasts.
discuss	**Share thoughts!** Talk about the topic as if you were sharing your knowledge with other people. Use details and examples to explain the topic.

explain	Tell me more! Make it clear! Provide the meaning, give your interpretation, and make it simple so the reader will understand. Create examples with details, procedures, or attributes. Give clear descriptions of the event, object, concept, or idea based on what you know.
identify	**Label and name it!** Give definitions and attributes of a person, place, event, or thing that make it unique. Describe the shape, size, color, and other defining characteristics.
interpret	**What does this mean?** Write your understanding of the passage in your own words. Ask yourself, "What does this _____ mean?" Give a view from your experiences and the information you find. Analyze the passage and report your opinion of the data.
list	**Jot it down! Brainstorm!** Write each item that applies to the topic or subject. This is a way to get your thoughts down quickly, to gather and group information.
outline	**ORDER, ORDER, order!** Outlines organize important data or information in a logical way using sequential steps. A formal outlining pattern uses roman numerals for major topics. Letters are used to identify details under each roman numeral. *Example:* I, A, B, 1, 2, a, b; II, and so on. Informal outlining organizes data or information in a logical way using sequential steps or procedures. *Example:* First I _____. Next I _____.
plot	**Organize the data!** Place the information on an organizer. Use a graphic design, a grid, a picture, a chart, or a matrix. These activities organize thoughts, consolidate information, and simplify topics.
summarize	**Sum it up!** Give the meaning in a concise way using as few words as possible. Ask yourself, "What is the author saying?" Retell the most important facts, the essential details, or the conclusion. Use the key points to give the overall picture of the author's meaning.
trace	**Follow the trail!** Place events, experiences, or thoughts in the order they occurred. A mental or written timeline is useful to see the chain of events.

Portfolios

A *content portfolio* is a special place to save work samples in a unit of focus. The materials chosen show evidence of the learner's progress, strengths, and needs.

Provide each student with a file or accordion folder to use as a subject area portfolio. Decorate the cover to represent the unit of study and the student. The design makes the portfolio easy to recognize and saves time when they are being distributed.

1. Include a list of the portfolio's content with the entry date for each item. The same title with the date is placed on the actual piece of work.

2. Create a skill list with space for additions. The teacher or the student adds new skills to the list as he learns how to apply them. He marks the skills that need more work. The list serves as a reminder for future needs and practice.

3. If the student chooses the topic, he needs a place to include a brain-storming list of ideas to write about later.

4. Work samples represent the student's "Best Work." The work is unique according to the learner's abilities and performances.

Portfolio Reflections

The following comments may be placed on a portfolio selection as a reflection piece. The comments may be written on sticky notes and attached to the work.

1. I decided to write this piece because _____.

2. I took a risk by_____.

3. I learned _____.

4. This was like an experiment because _____.

5. The next time I write I will _____.

6. This is a good piece of writing because _____.

Portfolio Conference Guide

The portfolio conference guide assists the listening partner as he analyzes and discusses the samples. The partners make suggestions and find possible problems and the pair develop workable solutions. The partner is an effective listener and lets the author lead the discussion. A listening partner may choose statements or questions from the following list to plan and use a portfolio conference:

1. Tell me about this selection.

2. What part did you like best?

3. I like the ____.

4. Do you have enough information to answer the problem or complete the assignment?

5. Why did you choose to write about this topic? (if it was a choice)

6. How does this writing compare to other pieces you have written?

7. This part is not clear to me. Will you explain it?

8. What could you do to make this work better?

9. Does the beginning grab the reader's attention?

10. Are you happy with the beginning/the ending?

11. Do you need to improve your work in some way?

12. Is your paper in the right order?

13. What do you need to add or delete?

14. Did you stick to the topic throughout your writing?

   Others _____

Portfolio Conference Form

The student needs time to complete a portfolio conference form before a partner discussion session begins. The following sample of a report form is a guide for the student to use when leading a portfolio conference with a peer:

1. Personal Identification Data
   Student _____ Class Period _____
   Date of Gathering: From _____ to _____
   Unit/Topic _____ Teacher _____

2. Table of Content Entries: List each work sample in the portfolio's table of contents. Use the title for the work and the date it was completed. Students should identify each entry as completed or work in progress.

3. Place two lines or boxes at the end of each entry on the list. Check the first box when the partner sees the work. He checks the second box when the discussion is completed.

   EXAMPLE

   (a) Editorial Cartoon   Completed 5/14/03   ❑   ❑

   (b) Journal Entry   ❑   ❑

Note: Usually it is unnecessary to discuss all pieces of the portfolio. Specific portfolio samples are assigned by the teacher or chosen by the student for discussions.

4. Provide a comment section for the portfolio conference.

    EXAMPLE

    What did you learn from the conference?
    Author
    Partner

5. The Signature Section is provided so partners take responsibility for following conference procedures and staying on task.

    EXAMPLE

    Author's Signature _____ Date _____

    Partner's Signature _____ Date _____

Differentiating the Writing Process

4

When a butterfly emerges from the cocoon,
he spreads his wings and flies.
When a student automatically uses writing skills
and strategies, he soars as a young author.

FLEXIBLE GROUPING

In the differentiated classroom, flexible groupings are essential to meet the diverse needs of learners and writers. In planning content-related writing experiences, the teacher assesses the students' learning styles and preferences. He selects the most effective grouping design to meet the personal needs of each student. Consider the following questions:

- How will the student work best to meet his physical and emotional needs?
- How does the student need to work to accomplish the task and reach his potential?

Teachers may use total groups to teach some lessons. The lessons may call for the student to work with others in small groups or partners. Partner groupings often are omitted in planning. Think of the active involvement that takes place as half of the students are engaged in talking or writing about the information at the same time. Partner and small group assignments promote discussion, teaming, and sharing. As a self-directed learner, the student needs to be an active participant in a variety of working scenarios. The appropriate grouping for each writing opportunity makes the difference in the success of that activity.

TAPS

Writing activities are completed with the **T**otal Group (T), with students working **A**lone (A), with **P**artner work (P), or with a **S**mall Group (S). The TAPS acronym, designed by Gregory and Chapman (2001), sends the message that teachers need to select the most effective grouping design so that it TAPS into each student's potential for a particular learning scene. Remember to plan writing groups according to the student's learning styles, intelligences, and writing personality (see Chapter 2). Keep in mind that students who get along socially can get the job done.

Figure 4.1 contains suggested designs for specific writing activities. Activities may be appropriate for more than one design.

Total Group

Use total group presentations when the entire class needs to hear the information in a consistent manner. For example, if students need to receive the same set of guidelines, rules, or directions, they need to hear all the information in the same way. In a lecturette, the teacher gives students the common topic information they need. Often a class discussion or guided practice is interwoven with the teacher's information. At times individuals or small groups report on a specific segment of the topic, share a report, or present a project. The total group should hear these learning celebrations.

Alone

Self-directed learners are able to process information alone, seek help from others when needed, and adapt learned information in their long-term memory banks. The students must have a personal link or need for the information. Students who are strong in intrapersonal intelligence learn best when they work alone. They need to work with others, however, to develop social skills. Authors need to work alone on some assignments. Usually writing is completed independently in the real world.

Partner

Some teachers ask, "Why do I need to ask students to work with a partner?" It has been the norm to place students in groups of threes or fours for

Figure 4.1   Flexible Grouping In the Differentiated Writing Classroom

Group Designs	Writing Tasks
Total Group	Brainstorming Making class lists Copying information Creating graffiti boards Creating word walls Completing KWL charts Making timelines Responding to learning Completing direction charts Compiling rules Plotting on a graphic organizer Reporting Taking notes Writing directions Guided practice Writing on chalkboards Writing on overheads Creating charts Writing facts graffiti style Writing on dry erase boards
Alone	Brainstorming Taking tests Solving a problem Taking notes Gathering research data Responding to learning Recording in journals Answering questions Plotting on a graphic organizer Answering open-ended questions Completing independent assignments Recording in logs and diaries Processing reflections Completing homework Participating in center activity
Partner	Brainstorming Conferencing with portfolios Peer-to-peer tutoring Responding to learning Recording data Recording information Plotting on a graphic organizer Revising and editing Researching Completing cooperative learning assignments Peer evaluations
Small Groups	Brainstorming Problem solving Designing posters Charting learning responses Making a group response sheet Taking notes Plotting on a graphic organizer Revising and editing Working in cooperative learning assignment Gathering research Assessing

group work. Many assignments work better with two students. Partner work provides more opportunity for each student to be actively engaged and participate. Think about it! During a writing assignment, if partners pass a paper back and forth between them, each one is writing, thinking, discussing, sharing answers, and responding during half of the assignment.

Also, some students prefer to work alone. They need to learn to work with people. It is easier for these students to work with a partner than to work in a group of three or four classmates.

Small Group

A student learns from conversation with other individuals. By discussing, sharing, and creating together, an effective small group pulls on the individual talents of the team members to complete the assignment successfully. Often the student who enjoys learning with other people is referred to as a social butterfly. He is strong in his interpersonal intelligence. This student processes information by sharing and finding listening ears.

IMMERSE STUDENTS IN THE WRITER'S CRAFT

Within their flexible groups, students are introduced to the many different forms of writing appropriate to different content areas. They move through the six steps of the writing process and immerse themselves in the writer's craft.

A *craft* is an art or skill. Writing specialist Katie Wood Ray (1999) emphasizes the value of teaching students the author's craft. This includes where authors obtain information, how they conduct research, and how they create drafts. Teachers and students must understand and practice these "how to's" of writing. Learners must know how to apply them effectively in all of the content areas.

The young authors need to develop a writing vocabulary with which to discuss their writing. These terms include *draft, revise, edit,* and *publish.* They become familiar with the language of writing through sharing and discussing their work. Invite local authors to share their work and advice with students to give the students meaningful connections to the vocabulary of the writer's craft.

TYPES OF WRITING

Four types of writing are presented in this section, with suggested teaching guidelines for each one. Teach students to use the sentence that follows the heading for each type of writing to guide his understanding and self-talk as he works with each one.

Descriptive Writing: Let Me Create a Picture in Your Mind!

Descriptive writing uses words to create picture images or impressions of a person, place, concept, object, or event. The student chooses his words for the mind's eye. The writer needs to grow in his ability to use descriptive language. This learning process develops over time through extensive practice and purposeful instruction within units of study. Begin descriptive writing experiences with simple assignments that ask the student to describe familiar things from his environment. It will be easier for the student to apply this skill to personal experiences because feelings and emotions reflect in these activities. Other types of writing use some elements of descriptive writing. (For tips on writing with style, see the Step 3. Hamming It Up: Revision section later in the chapter.)

To use descriptive writing, the learner must

- Use adjectives, adverbs, and verbs effectively
- Understand how words activate the senses
- Give actions to characters and objects
- Use words to express and share ideas
- Create pictures and images in the reader's mind

EXAMPLES OF DESCRIPTIVE WRITING FORMS

Character analysis   Eyewitness accounts
Poetic descriptions   Comparisons/Contrasts

Expository Writing: Let Me Explain It to You!

Expository writing informs with an explanation or report. It may involve giving a step-by-step account or a "how to" procedure. The causes of an event may be revealed. Expository writing is found in training books, in assembly manuals, in recounts or explanations of an event, or in the retelling of a story. Key words used in some expository writing include *first*, *second*, *then*, *next*, and *finally*.

To use expository writing, the learner must

- Know the meaning of *informing* and *explaining*
- Remember the order of an event, procedure, or process
- Be specific and accurate in explanations
- Write for readers who may retell the information or follow the procedure step by step

EXAMPLES OF EXPOSITORY WRITING FORMS

Book report   Directions   Research paper
How-to guide   Instructions   News story
Recount of an event

Persuasive Writing: Let Me Convince You!

Persuasive writing is the author's attempt to change the beliefs or behaviors of an individual or group of people. The writer uses words and phrases to convince the reader or audience that new ideas or changes should be adapted.

The author states his opinion and provides facts and details that explain, prove, or support his opinion. The conclusion summarizes or restates the writer's beliefs. Students enjoy expressing opinions and ideas, so persuasive writing is an excellent tool to use when processing information. For example, young authors enjoy inventing new ways to use objects or ideas and creating persuasive passages to sell the products.

To use persuasion in writing, the learner must

- Know how to state his opinions and beliefs
- Understand that his words can change or "sway" the beliefs of his readers
- Become aware of personal feelings and the beliefs of other people
- Demonstrate logical thinking and problem-solving skills in making decisions
- Realize that ideas, beliefs, rules, and laws can change by rewriting phrases, sentences, or sections

EXAMPLES OF PERSUASIVE WRITING FORMS

Book reviews	Brochures	Commercials	Business letters
Editorials	Movie reviews	Posters	Letters to the Editor

Narrative Writing: Let Me Tell You What Happened!

A narrative tells a story. It may be about an event in the present, past, or future. It may be fiction or nonfiction. The story may be in various forms, including diaries, chapter books, short stories, essays, plays, tall tales, or legends.

To use narrative writing, the learner must

- Know how to tell a story
- Write as if he is telling the story to someone.
- Develop a beginning to introduce the characters, scene, and problem
- Develop characters and actions throughout the story
- Create an ending that gives the problem, solution, or conclusion

EXAMPLES OF NARRATIVE WRITING FORMS

Biographies	Diaries	Fantasies	Fables	Historical fiction
Legends	Mysteries	Myths	Novels	Current events
Short stories	Plays	Stories	Sitcoms	Science fiction

Figure 4.2 Types of Writing

Descriptive Writing Purpose: To picture Features • Uses adjectives, adverbs, and sensory words and active verbs • Shows instead of tells • Uses imagery, metaphors, and similes • Creates mental pictures Examples • Describe a place, person, object, or event. • Visualize a picture in one's mind. • Write a story, poem, report, or essay.	**Expository Writing** Purpose: To inform Features • Recounts or retells using who, what, when, where, and why • Gives details • Shows or tells step by step • Describes a procedure • Explains "how to" Examples • Tell what happened for a news program. • Record the event in a diary. • Explain the procedure. • Retell the story. • Write a manual, procedure, recipe, or news flash.
Narrative Writing Purpose: To tell Features • Gives details of characters, plot, setting, and events • Tells who, what, when, and where • Has a strong story line • Shows sequence of events • States problems, complications, or dilemmas • Defines or tells about _____. Examples • Tell about an event, place, person, or thing for a newspaper. • Write a story (fact or fiction) for a school newspaper.	**Persuasive Writing** Purpose: To convince Features • Strives to change the audience's thoughts and ideas • States a point of view • Tells what and why • Has a specific audience • Gives the expert's and believer's side • States position with support • Contains a closing argument Examples • Convince the audience that_____ for a speech. • Write an editorial to express your feelings about_____. • Write an article to win the reader over to your side of an issue in a brochure.

Figure 4.2 summarizes the purposes and features of the four types of writing and gives assignment examples.

THE BLOCK PARTY

The Block Party activity is designed to meet the diverse needs of students as they practice the four types of writing. It is also an effective activity for practicing the writing process. Assign responsibilities and roles using the students' learning preferences and their areas of strength related to their intelligences. You will need the following materials: one sheet of chart paper for each group; Cool Tools, including marking pens and one index card, for each group. Each student will need his own paper, pen, and booklet, and several small pieces of paper.

Begin by assigning each student a partner. The steps that follow are performed by the students.

Part I

1. Take your paper, pen, and booklet to meet your partner.

2. Join with another set of partners to form your Block Party, which is made up of four individuals.

3. Choose a Captain and a Materials Person.

4. The Captain
   - Obtains one piece of chart paper
   - Folds the chart paper to create four equal sections
   - Uses a marker to outline the four sections

5. As a team, select one noun for the Captain to write on an index card. The noun may be a person, animal, event, object, or place.

6. Place the noun card in the center of the chart. The chart will serve as a graphic organizer for the brainstorming that follows in Part III.

Part II

1. The Materials Person writes the letters *D, E, P,* and *N*—to represent the four types of writing—on four small pieces of paper, one letter on each piece. He wads the slips of paper into a ball.

2. Each team member draws a piece of paper from the ball. The letter tells the individual his or her assigned block on the chart.

3. Each team member writes the type of writing he's drawn in his block. For example, the student who draws an *N* writes "Narrative" in his block. He will be responsible for recording the brainstormed ideas on the graphic organizer in the "Narrative" block.

Part III

Students in each Block Party brainstorm information for the four types of writing. The teacher gives the directions for each block.

Block 1   Descriptive Writing

   1. Draw a Sunshine Web. (A *Sunshine Web* is a circle with lines extending from it for rays.)

   2. Write the noun chosen in the center.

   3. On each ray, place an attribute of the noun using a descriptive word or phrase to describe the subject.

Note: Remind participants that the person with the letter for each block will record responses from the group on the organizer for his section. Each member brainstorms response for each block.

Block 2   Expository Writing

   1. List words or phrases about the noun to use in a newspaper ad.

   2. Write the list in graffiti style using colored markers or pens.

Block 3   Persuasive Writing

   1. Draw a hand shape in the center of the block.

   2. Write the noun in the palm of the hand.

   3. On each finger tell why the noun is "the best."

Block 4   Narrative Writing

   1. Draw five boxes in the block.

   2. Inside the five boxes write the five W's of narrative writing, with one word in each box: *Who, What, When, Where,* and *Why*.

   3. Answer and write each *W* in relation to the noun, using words and phrases.

Part IV

Find a comfortable place to write one or more paragraphs using the type of writing identified in your block. Use the ideas recorded on the chart to complete your writing activity. Follow these directions for your type of writing:

Descriptive Writing: Describe your noun for a special exhibit or event.

Expository Writing: Write an ad for the noun to appear in the local newspaper.

Persuasive Writing: Convince judges that your noun should win an award.

Narrative Writing: Write a paragraph about the noun that includes the five W's.

Note to teachers: Remind the authors that they are using the group's brainstorming, a *prewriting* activity. They are now *drafting,* the second step in the writing process.

Part V

1. Return to your Block Party.

2. Take turns sharing the writing with the Block Party group.

Optional: Lead the authors into the revision and editing steps of the writing process.

3. Choose one example from your Block Party to share with the total group. Call on each Block Party to share the activity for a type of writing.

Celebrate!

THE WRITING PROCESS

The writing process provides simple, sequential steps for the writer to use. The common titles for the steps are *prewriting, drafting, revising, editing, final copy,* and *publishing*. It is not necessary to take a student through all steps in the process in every writing activity. The purpose of a writing activity may be simply to get the information down on paper. In other words, the objective of the activity may be for the learner to use writing to stimulate thinking and reflection. In this case, the act of writing is the product. For example, the student may complete the first draft and share it.

Process the Process

Students need to know and understand the steps in the writing process. Teach the name of each step, so the words become a part of the learners' vocabulary. Use the same terminology each time the step is used. Require the students to use the appropriate terms when engaged in conversations and activities related to the writing process. They need opportunities to rehearse the words often and in many ways, so they can automatically use them in their writing vocabulary.

One forgets words as one forgets names. One's vocabulary needs constant fertilizing or it will die.

—Evelyn Waugh, British novelist

Practice the Process

The following song, "I'm an Author," is used to teach students the steps in the Writing Process. One verse may be used as each step is introduced.

"I'M AN AUTHOR"

(Sung to the tune, "Are You Sleeping?")

Prewriting! Prewriting!
Gather thoughts, get data.
Pull my thoughts together.
This is my time to think.
Brainstorming! Brainstorming!

Revising! Revising!
Work on the words. Reorganize.
Give it style. Add pizzazz.
Ham it up! Ham it up!

Final Copy! Final Copy!
Add all changes. Write it neatly.
Make it clear.
This is called a rewrite.
Neat Sheet! Neat Sheet!

Drafting! Drafting!
Write it down. Don't skip words.
Organize ideas.
This is my first draft.
Sloppy Copy! Sloppy Copy!

Editing! Editing!
Check capital letters.
Spell words correctly.
Correct punctuation.
These are the mechanics.
Tune it up! Tune it up!

Publishing! Publishing!
Share my writing. Display it now!
I'm a proud author.
I'm a published author.
Celebrate! Celebrate!

—(Chapman & King, 2003)

Here are more activities to help students learn the sequence of the steps in the writing process:.

- Write the steps in graffiti style on banners, mobiles, and bulletin boards.
- Sing the steps to a familiar tune.
- Rap the steps to a catchy beat.

- Create a design with the name of each step.
- Write a cheer to use with each step.

STEP 1. GETTING STARTED: PREWRITING

Prewriting is the time to prepare for writing. It is the step before the first draft of the product. If prewriting is used correctly, students are eager and prepared to write. Prewriting experiences create the students' desire to write about specific topics. A prewriting session is provided for the learner to get hooked into the activity, to gather data, and to organize thoughts related to the information.

Teacher's Role for the Prewriting Step

Introduce the prewriting assignment to the student, so he knows the answers to questions such as, "What is it?" "Why am I writing?" "What is the purpose of this assignment?" and "Who will be in my audience?"

Set expectations with specific purposes for the writing experience. Share the criteria to answer questions the student may unconsciously ask, such as, "What is in this assignment for me?" or "Why should I complete this assignment?" Motivate the learner. He must understand the criteria and see a need to complete the activity. To meet this challenge, keep the assignment alive and exciting.

Create an atmosphere of wonder through anticipation, surprise, and fascination in relation to the topic. Use curiosity to focus the learner's attention on the information and stimulate his thinking. For example, if the teacher assumed the role of a soldier in the Civil War, the student will say, "I wonder what he'll think of next!"

Identify the audience that will hear or read the writer's thoughts. The audience may be the author, a partner, a small group, or a large group. An audience may be fictitious or factual. Teach the student to select his audience and write as if he is talking to the person or group of people. Vary the audience to add novelty to the lessons.

Hook them during prewriting experiences. Hooks are motivating activities designed to intrigue, challenge, and focus attention on the writing experience. Hooks play on the senses. They build interest, evoke curiosity, and stir the imagination. A hook is effective when a student cannot wait to put his pencil to the paper.

Discover what the students <u>K</u>now, <u>W</u>ant to know, and <u>L</u>earn (KWL). Uncover the students' knowledge about a topic before planning lessons. Find out what they know, what they want to know, and what they are learning. It will be helpful to know what they do not like or do not want to explore. Link the topic to the students' past experiences. They need to know the subject's relationship to their personal knowledge. These connections will stimulate their desire to learn more.

Use brainstorming, listing, and note taking to discover the components for KWL. A Language Experience activity is an effective tool to use for this purpose, too. Record the student's thoughts and ideas on chart paper, the board, an overhead transparency, or a computer-projected screen. These experiences may be conducted with a Total group, Alone, with a Partner, or as a Small group activity.

Choose an appropriate graphic organizer to match the information. For instance, if the study involves insects, use an outline of a bug. If the study is about space, use an outline of a rocket. The organizer categorizes and arranges the author's ideas, so he concentrates on the flow of his ideas related to the content. The first draft is easier to complete when ideas are gathered and recorded on a graphic organizer.

Vary assignment strategies to gather the information. A student may follow a step-by-step procedure to collect the data he needs. In other assignments, he may use his own procedure. The student needs varied ways to complete his work. He may need to discuss the topic with others. The learner may work better alone. Provide opportunities for the student to work with others and time for him to work alone. Strategically vary assignments throughout the plans, so the student will use different strategies to complete the tasks. Variety is the key!

Teacher Checklist for Prewriting Preparation

Strategically plan prewriting experiences. Here are some decisions to consider during preparations for prewriting:

1. Select the topic or create a list of topic choices.

2. Decide if the writing assignment will be informal or formal.

3. Choose an intriguing strategy or activity to "hook" students on the topic.

4. Determine the length of the assignment.

5. Select the form for the author to use. *Examples:* Song, play, or list.

6. Select the reading or listening audience.

7. Determine the purpose of the writing assignment. *Examples:* To share with a partner, to create test study notes, or to publish.

8. Select the type of paper to use. *Examples:* Unlined, textured, or a shape.

9. Choose the writing instruments. *Examples:* Pencil, pen, marker.

10. Decide the length of time the student needs for the writing activity. *Examples:* One class period, homework, a week.

Prewriting Guidelines

After decisions and plans are made for the prewriting stage, use the following guidelines during the experience:

1. Set the tone for the writing experience.

2. Give clear specific directions and guidelines.

3. Check the learner's understanding of the assignment.

4. Provide time for the author to collect his thoughts.

5. Ask open-ended questions.

6. Be a listener. Probe and jog the student's mind for ideas.

7. Pose a thinking problem. Examples: What would you do if _____?

8. Encourage the student to pool all of his thoughts about _____.

9. Build a spirit of helpfulness by encouraging the student to share information and ideas.

10. Model or demonstrate various ways the student may assist someone.

11. Ask the student to restate the assignment.

12. Show your enthusiasm!

A Baker's Dozen: An Author's Self-Talk Guide for Prewriting

(A "baker's dozen" has thirteen items because an extra item is included as bonus or a gift!)

Before writing action begins, complete the following checklist:

1. My assignment is _____.

2. I need to _____.

3. The topic of my writing will be _____.

4. When I think about this subject, I already know _____.

5. The best genre to use to share my ideas is _____.

6. I could gather more information from the library, interviews, or the Internet.

7. My reader or audience will be _____.

8. My role for this piece of writing is _____

   Examples: A character? A bystander? A storyteller?

9. I may have a problem with _____.

10. My purpose for writing this selection is _____.

11. The hardest part of this writing will be _____.

12. The easiest part of this writing will be _____.

13. When I write, I _____.

Idea Round-Up: Crucial Collections

The collection of data and ideas about a topic is crucial for prewriting. Data includes all information needed for the writing activity. The collection time is more important for some writing assignments than others.

Vary the gathering techniques. The student may know a lot about a topic from personal experiences, but he needs time to collect thoughts and write notes. The notes are used to organize what he wants to say. Reports or informational essays require more data. As facts are collected, the student learns more about the subject.

How is data collected? Many avenues exist for a student to search for information and ideas. Teach the young author how to use various collection tools. When he uses the strategies independently, encourage him to choose the most beneficial collection strategy for his activity.

COLLECTION SELECTIONS

The following list has suggested resources to collect information:

Books	Brainstorming	Charts	Concept maps	Drawings
Dreams	Experiences	Articles	Imagination	Internet
Interviews	Journals	Listening	Movies	Observations
Questions	Quotations	Plays	Television shows	Thoughts

(Also see the Gathering Research section in Chapter 5.)

Curriculum Compacting

A student may demonstrate in the prewriting step that he is in the high level of mastery. If he has an in-depth knowledge of the topic, teachers may provide individual, alternative projects and assignments such as *curriculum compacting*. Joseph Renzulli (Renzulli & Reis, 1998) developed a well-known curriculum compacting model. In this approach the curriculum is differentiated to provide extended or expanded activities. The student uses a form to record the topic he will study and a description of the activities or project he will complete with the sources. He submits the form to the teacher for approval.

The learner may choose to research a subtopic so he can go into more depth. He is not required to spend his time studying information he already knows. Curriculum compacting differentiates instruction by challenging and motivating individual students to learn more.

Example

Contract Form

Name_____   Date_____

Subject_____   Teacher _____

Plan:

I need to write about this topic because _____.

I will use the following resources: _____.

My writing will be presented in the form of a _____.

(journal, play, radio show, PowerPoint presentation, magazine article)

Student Signature _____

Teacher Signature_____

STEP 2. SLOPPY COPY: FIRST DRAFT

The goal of this step of the writing process is to get down on paper the thoughts that were gathered during the prewriting stage. The author writes his words freely as if he were telling someone the information. Sometimes a writer gets "writer's block" when he is concerned with correct spelling or making grammatical errors. This hampers the author's flow of ideas. Strongly recommend the use of invented spelling in the draft. This keeps the writer from stopping and losing his train of thought. Tell the student to concentrate on the content and organization for his work. Remind him that spelling and mechanical errors are corrected in later stages of the writing process.

Teacher's Role in the First Draft

Create a positive climate that is a nonthreatening environment in which students feel free to take risks. Encourage students to find a comfortable spot to write their first draft. Use positive comments and words of encouragement. Expect successful experiences!

Model being a writer. Teachers need to write with the students so that everyone is writing during the first-draft stage. Learners need to hear the teacher's enthusiasm and excitement before drafting begins and as writing is shared. They need to hear the work of well-known authors who use various writing styles, areas of interest, and genres.

Believe students can write. Students should say and believe, "If I can say it, I can write it!" They need to understand that writing is the author's "talk written down." The following statements keep students focused on placing their thoughts on paper: "Pretend you are telling this information to someone standing beside you. Talk to that person and write each word exactly like you are saying it. Do not skip a word or thought." When writers learn to use this strategy, believe in their ability, and use it, they are better writers.

Encourage invented spelling. Invented spelling uses the sounds of letters to spell. This phonetic spelling enhances creative writing. When phonetic spelling is accepted in free writing and first drafts, the student has more freedom to record his thoughts without concern for correctness. Emphasis on correct spelling interferes with the learner's concentration on content and organization during first draft writing. Remember, a student's speaking and writing vocabulary is larger than his spelling vocabulary.

The author is asked to read his own writing because invented spelling is easily misinterpreted. For example, if the student writes, "ilikmihos," it could be interpreted as "I like my house" or "I like my horse." A student who is free to use invented spelling uses more words with multiple syllables because he can spell them phonetically. For example, he may write "klorafil" for chlorophyll and "fotosinthesis" for photosynthesis. He can pronounce the word as he reads his own writing to describe the color-changing process of leaves.

The first draft emphasizes the importance of focusing on recording content ideas and organization. Spelling corrections are made later in the editing stage of the writing process after thoughts are placed on paper. The words a student spells correctly in the first-draft writing are the student's mastered words. The learner spells these words automatically. This means that first-draft writing provides an assessment tool to analyze mastered spelling words, grammar, and punctuation.

It may be difficult to make decisions related to spelling expectations during writing activities. Language arts specialists have debated spelling requirements in writing activities for many years. The latest research overwhelmingly supports invented spelling in first-draft writing. Students are more creative with their writing ideas when invented spelling is accepted.

Spelling Guidelines for Writing Activities These research-based suggestions are related to invented spelling. They are presented to assist teachers with spelling guidelines for writing activities.

• The first draft is the Sloppy Copy. The emphasis is not on correct spelling during first-draft writing. During this step in the writing process, the author focuses his attention on the content and organization of the information.

• If the author spells a word correctly or uses a grammar rule accurately, the skill is mastered. Assess the writing to identify spelling skills to emphasize during instruction.

• The writer needs to know that spelling corrections are made when he edits the work. The following response may be made to a student when he asks the teacher to spell a word correctly in the first draft: "Listen to sounds in the word, then spell it your way." The student needs assurance that misspelled words are accepted. The author needs to be reminded not to omit a word, substitute another word, or use a smaller word because he cannot spell it correctly. This technique should be modeled several times because students may not be accustomed to leaving mistakes in their work. Routinely remind students that their ideas are more important than correct spelling in the first writing stages.

• The student needs to complete more first drafts than later steps in the writing process. If he has to go through every step of the process with every paper he writes, he will be "turned off" to writing. The author must focus on the topic and use prewriting ideas during this step. A paper does not need to go through several revisions. The writer needs more Sloppy Copies than Neat Sheets because he learns to write by writing!

Note! Phonics is more widely taught today than it was in the past decade. In the future, a student will have more background knowledge to use invented spelling.

Figure 4.3 shows the readiness level of certain groups of students in the classroom. It identifies the information the students at these three levels need to learn. The learners at each level of mastery are in that category because of their personal experiences and backgrounds. Each level represents the individual knowledge base of students on a particular topic, skill, or standard.

Figure 4.3   Adjustable Assignment for Invented Spelling

B • Give specific praise • Encourage spelling of multisyllable words • Needs to read his own writing	• Needs to build confidence and security • Needs reassurance that incorrect spelling will not be graded • Needs praise for independent attempts to tackle unfamiliar words	• Needs teacher modeling of strategy • Needs to learn the strategies and techniques for invented spelling • Needs to hear the step-by-step thinking needed to spell words phonetically • Needs more phonics background • Needs to learn rules and how to apply them
A • Is eager to express himself in writing • Is secure and confident to make spelling attempts • Has a strong phonics background • Understands that invented spelling enhances flow of thought • Knows how to use invented spelling automatically in the first draft	• Tries to spell words independently • Has some phonetic background • Uses invented spelling occasionally • Insecure with the process • Asks for assistance when spelling difficult words	• Does not have a strong phonetic background • Does not understand invented spelling techniques • "Shuts down" • Does not write the words he is thinking and saying • Asks for assistance
High Degree of Mastery	**Approaching Mastery**	**Beginning Mastery**

Standard: To be able to use invented spelling
Key: A. What do they know now?
       B. What do they need to learn next?

The Drafting Craft: Guidelines for Students

To create my first draft, I need to

1. ___ Find a comfortable place to think and write
2. ___ Skip lines for revising and editing

3. ___ Use my prewriting notes, ideas, and organizers
4. ___ Pretend I am telling the story to someone standing beside me
5. ___ Write every word without skipping or omitting a word
6. ___ Include new ideas that come to me as I write
7. ___ Use the punctuation marks I know how to use automatically
8. ___ Spell words the way they sound, because I have permission to use invented spelling
9. ___ Read the first draft to myself; I am the only one who needs to be able to read the first draft
10. ___ Read my completed first draft to a peer, a small group, or the teacher

Off to a Smart Start: Beginning the First Draft

Use attention getters for openers! The first part of the passage must grab the reader's attention, pique curiosity, and stir interest, so it entices the reader to keep reading.

Involve the emotions and senses. Ask a profound question to build curiosity. Also, remember to use detailed descriptions to set the plot, describe the scene, and create the characters.

Try these ideas after prewriting, as the writer begins the first draft. An idea is refined or improved during the revision step.

- Choose a unique, quality beginning.
- Add details with questions, strong verbs, and adjectives.
- Read the passage to decide if the piece needs more or less information.
- Refine the work and then reread it.

Publishing Drafts

It is not necessary for all writing to go through the entire publishing process. When drafts are displayed, announce that the work is not revised or edited. Inform audiences of the first draft that punctuation, capitalization, and other mechanics of writing are not the major focus in this step of the work.

SUGGESTED DISPLAY SPACES FOR DRAFTS

- Author's book or folder
- Centers
- Bulletin boards
- Clotheslines
- Ribbons/Ropes
- Charts

DISPLAY DRAFTS WITH SIGNS SIMILAR TO THE FOLLOWING:

- First Draft Writing
- Writing Under Construction
- Draft Craft
- *Work in Progress*

Create Interest

Teach students the value of making the writing interesting and enjoyable for their audiences. They must learn how to grab and maintain their readers' attention. Use the following guidelines to create interest.

- Surprise with an unusual format or genre.
- Tell it from a unique point of view.
- Compare or contrast with a familiar event, person, or object.
- Match the readers' needs.
- Stir the readers' curiosity.
- Pose a question.
- Use fascinating facts.
- Use personification.
- Generate a feeling of happiness.
- Stimulate the readers' senses.
- Stir emotions.
- Use a surprise ending.

Clear Away the Cobwebs

New ideas are easier to weave when thoughts are clear, so it may be necessary to remove mental cobwebs. Students need to understand the value of putting their work out of sight for a period of time. The time away from writing will provide a mental escape and clear the cobwebs from their minds. They usually have new, fresh ideas when they return to their writing. Folders designed for writing experiences or units of study provide handy storage places to use as the cobwebs clear.

Conferencing Guidelines for Reviewing First Drafts

The following guidelines are suggested for students to use during draft conferences:

1. Raise your hand when you complete your first draft.

2. Wait for the teacher to assign you a partner.

3. Choose a comfortable place to work together.

4. Take a pencil, because revisions will begin during your first reading.

5. Read your writing aloud to your partner. As you read, correct obvious errors including omitted words, extra words, capitalization, and punctuation.

6. Discuss the selection with your partner.

7. Take notes on your partner's suggestions.

8. Consider your partner's suggestions for corrections and improvements.

When students use writing mechanics correctly in first-draft writing, the skills have been mastered.

> *Like butterflies freed from cages . . .*
> *Thoughts fly from my mind*
> *Filling many pages.*
>
> —Chapman & King, 2003

STEP 3. HAMMING IT UP: REVISION

> I rewrote the ending to *Farewell to Arms,* the last page of it, thirty-nine times, before I was satisfied.
>
> —Ernest Hemingway

The revision step in the writing process organizes the content, makes additions, and deletes unnecessary information. The author checks the flow of ideas, the organization, conveyance, and intent of the message. As the author reads, the listener needs to understand the message. Style is added at this step. The work is reviewed for corrections. The author evaluates his work and makes corrections. He works to move the writing toward perfection.

Teacher's Role in Revision

Choose appropriate opportunities for revision. All writing assignments do not go through the revising process. Students need to practice getting their ideas on paper many times, so complete the prewriting and drafting steps often. Assign revisions selectively. Remember, if the student revises every assignment, he will be less motivated to write.

Allow the student to select a piece of work to revise. Each student does not have to revise the same product in the first-draft assignment. For best results, ask the author to choose a first-draft selection from his topic folder or notebook. The author will be more interested in making revisions if he makes the selection. He will demonstrate his best work if he knows he is preparing the writing for a display or publication.

Make revisions on the first draft. Remind the student to use the lines he skipped in the first draft for his revisions. Use arrows, carats (^), and other symbols to indicate places to add and delete words or phrases. He will enjoy cutting and pasting phrases, sentences, and paragraphs to revise because these tasks are easier than rewriting.

Plan revision conferences. Revision conferences take place with a partner, small group, or the teacher. Revisions are the student's major responsibility, but the suggestions of others may be included. The author makes the final revision decisions. The revision process is time consuming, but the student needs to participate in conversations and dialogues about possible changes. Conferences provide opportunities for the student to talk and generate improvement ideas. Make this time a pleasant experience for everyone involved.

Determine the number of changes according to the student's needs. The writer may decide he is not able to write if too many revisions are cited. If the writer steeps in anger, he will turn off to writing experiences, so be aware of negative attitudes and frustrations. Avoid requirements for the author to correct every mistake. Each improvement to the writing is an indicator that the student is growing as an author. Revisions are designed to improve writing, not to perfect it.

In revision conferences, the author maintains control of corrections. If someone revises too much of his work, the author may feel that he no longer owns the writing.

Make revision a step in learning for the author. Revision suggestions may come from the author or other individuals. The author approves of each change and correction. If the author and editor disagree because the author wants to say it his way, the work remains as the author intended it. The author learns writing skills as he makes corrections.

Putting Style in Writing

Writing style is the way the individual writer states his or her ideas on paper. This style sets the writer apart from other writers. Each author has his own unique ideas and style. A writer may express himself with many words and details, while another author may use fewer words and less detail. Each approach reflects the author's individual style.

Style makes the writing unique! Just as a person dresses to fit his style, the author's originality and personality reflect in his writing. The following guidelines are designed for a student to use as he learns to implement style in his writing.

Add Adjectives

Use adjectives to describe the characters and the setting. Follow these suggested guidelines to add the special describing words:

1. Find important nouns in the first draft.

2. Place a carat (^) in front of each noun.

3. Add an adjective or adjectives to describe the noun.

4. Read the new sentence to your partner the old way and the new way.

5. Ask your partner to "give a thumbs up" if the phase is improved with the new adjective. Ask him to "give a thumbs down" if the adjective did not improve the phrase.

6. Decide if the changes are needed. (Each change is the author's decision.)

7. Make needed changes on your Sloppy Copy.

Add Adverbs

Adverbs add animation and detail to the verb, making the character, scenes, or events easier to visualize. Follow the suggested guidelines to add adverbs. Make a class list of adverbs on a visible chart.

1. Find important verbs in the first draft.

2. Place a carat (^) before or after the verb.

3. Add an adverb to describe the verb.

4. Read the new sentence to your partner the old way and the new way.

5. Ask your partner to "give a thumbs up" if the phase is improved with the new adverb. Ask your partner to "give a thumbs down" if the adverb does not improve the phrase.

6. As the author, you decide if the change is needed.

7. Make your changes on the Sloppy Copy.

Add WOW! Words

"WOW! Words" are words and phrases that end with an exclamation point. They express strong feelings and emotions from frustration to excitement. Make a chart of WOW! Words for the classroom. Have students generate words that require an exclamation point. Remind writers to add exclamations to dialogue. Find places in the writing to add WOW! Words on the Sloppy Copy.

EXAMPLES

Awesome!	Crash!	Bang!	Help!	Oh, no!	Duh!
Uh-oh!	Yeah!	Yes!	Yikes!	WOW!	Bad!

Oh, no! The native threw the boomerang.
Wow! The Incas were incredible builders.

Add Dialogue and Conversation

Dialogue evokes emotion and places the reader in the scene with the characters. When writing dialogue, avoid overuse of words. For instance, substitute words for *said* to show the characters' true feelings in conversations.

Instead of "Said"

Activity 1

Replace "said" with other action verbs. Create a class list of words to substitute for the word *said*. Tell the student to copy the list and place it in his writing folder as a reference tool.

EXAMPLES

cry	laugh	whimper	weep	squeal	yell	whisper	coo
yelp	gripe	complain	ridicule	gossip	confess	giggle	

Activity 2

Tell the student to look through a writing selection and draw a line through the word *said*. Ask him to write a word that reflects the character's emotion above the word *said*.

Activity 3

Ask the student to draw a happy face and write "happy" words for said around it or coming out of the mouth. Tell him to draw a sad face and write "sad" words around it. If the student needs an introduction to using the verb replacements, use the following activity:

Activity 4

Create cards with words to substitute for the word *said*.

1. Assign partners.

2. Each partner team draws a replacement word for *said*.

3. Partners select actions to role-play the word and practice.

4. Form a class circle.

5. Call on each partner team to display their word and role-play actions to describe the word.

6. Ask classmates to guess each word.

Vary Sentence Type

Teach the learner to write sentences in an inviting order, so readers clearly understand the meaning. Take the boredom out of a selection by varying the type of sentences.

- Put excitement and feelings in the plot with exclamatory sentences. *Examples:* Wow! Zing! What pizzazz!
- Use statements to tell or explain. Declarative sentences tell readers what you want them to know.
- Ask questions. Questions create curiosity. They make the reader think of a response or guess what comes next. Questions may indicate that an exciting answer will follow.
- Give a command, a direction, or an order occasionally.
- Check your work for variety with sentence beginnings, length, and style.

Use Figurative Language

Add flair and style by using figurative language such as similes, metaphors, and analogies.

Use the Mind's Eye

Teach the student to be conscious of the visual pictures or images in his mind. He will not be able to produce mental pictures unless he has had experiences that create them. For example, if the student writes about the Egyptian pyramids, he must have some knowledge of pyramids to produce the images.

The student's level of knowledge varies according to the depth of his experiences. The student who has a strong knowledge base on the subject has more descriptors for his writing. The student needs practice with describing words. Have the writer first draw a picture, then write about it. The illustration creates a concrete visual as a handy writing tool. Practice the use of describing words using familiar topics, such as a tree changing the color of its leaves.

Dig Deeper

When a student writes an inadequate amount of information, he needs to include more detail. He needs to "dig deeper" in the main idea or topic. For example, if the author has one or two sentences that stand alone, he needs to learn how to effectively elaborate or embellish his idea. Try the following strategy to help a student add needed detail to a passage.

1. Ask the author to read the sentences aloud.

2. Say, "Tell me more about _____."

3. Ask the student to write exactly the words he said. Remind him not to skip a word. The listener takes notes and leaves them with the author, so he can use them as a reference when he continues to write.

4. Guide the student to realize that writing is simply "talk written down" for someone to read or for the author to use later.

Note: Remember, it is easier for students to "tell it" than it is for them to "write it."

Key Marks for Revision

Use the following key as a handy tool to use for revisions. Teach the author how to use the key for self-monitoring or to prepare for a revision conference.

? I need to go back to this section for more work.

! This part is on target.

× This section may need to be deleted.

+ I need to add more information here.

Revision Conferences: Sharing the Work

Schedule a conference at this point in the writing process. The author reads his work orally to a partner, small groups, or the teacher. Rereading is a valuable skill to use in revision step (Fletcher & Portalupi, 1998), because the author receives specific suggestions for improvements from the listeners.

Teach students how to give suggestions to the writer in ways that improve the piece and maintain the author's feeling of ownership. Teach and reinforce the rules for productive sharing. Discuss and practice the rules for making suggestions.

Listener's Rules and Guidelines for Revisions

- Respect the author and the selection.
- Listen carefully.
- Ask specific questions.
- Make positive comments.
- Give constructive suggestions to make the paper better.

EXAMPLES

- I like _____ because _____.
- What is your favorite part?
- What do you think would make your writing better?
- How can I help you?

CONVERSATION LEAD-INS

- You could _____.
- Try adding _____.
- How would this sentence sound if _____.
- Try saying it this way: _____.
- Let's try _____.
- Read it without _____.
- Tell me more about _____.
- Explain the section _____.
- Let's move _____ to _____.

Share With a Partner or Small Group

The work is shared so the author hears the work and has someone's listening ear to provide feedback. The author reads his own paper to the audience.

When suggestions are accepted, the student internalizes skills as he actively applies them. This experience develops critical thinking and interpersonal skills. The author needs to know that the revision conference is designed to strengthen his writing sample.

Group Guidelines for Revisions

1. Choose a writing sample.

2. Join your partner or group with your writing sample and pencil.

3. Find a cozy place to work.

4. The author reads his selection to the audience or listener.

5. As you read, make changes on your Sloppy Copy.

EXAMPLES

Fill in omitted words . . .
Mark out unnecessary words.

6. Ask the listener to share his favorite parts.

7. Encourage the listener to make positive comments with specific suggestions.

8. Take turns sharing ideas to improve the writing.

9. The partners or group discuss each revision, but the writer has the final decision related to changes in the work.

Author's Discussion Prompts for Revisions

- What did you like about my writing?
- What would make this passage better?
- Do I need to leave out or add words, phrases, or sentences?
- Do I need to substitute a better word or phrase?
- Do I need to move a section?
- Do you have other suggestions to improve my work?

The author takes his notes or sample work and the conference suggestions, finds a quiet spot, and makes final revisions on the Sloppy Copy. When he has completed all revisions, he may use the following revision checklist as a reflection guide. The following checklist will identify areas that need more work in the writing, or it will indicate that the work is complete.

Author's Revision Checklist

The author may use the following checklist after the revision conference. The checklist is an effective reflection tool.

Check each statement as it is completed.

1. ___ I wrote what I was thinking.
2. ___ The beginning is interesting and hooks the reader.
3. ___ Important, accurate information is included.
4. ___ I tapped into the reader's senses with my descriptions.
5. ___ All sentences are clear, correct, and in order.
6. ___ I replaced simple words with more interesting words.
7. ___ The sentences have varied beginnings, length, and style.
8. ___ The details support the main idea.
9. ___ I added the words, phrases, or sentences that need to be added.
10. ___ I deleted words, phrases, or sentences that need to be removed.
11. ___ I moved parts of the story that need to move.
12. ___ I have an interesting closing.
13. ___ I am proud of my work!

Author's Self-Evaluation

The author uses a self-evaluation similar to the following before or after the conference or revisions.

1. ___ I have enough information.
2. ___ My work is interesting to read.
3. ___ The information is accurate.
4. ___ My report is informative.
5. ___ The writing is easy to read.
6. ___ The work sends the message I want to convey.
7. ___ I have considered all suggestions.
8. ___ I have given correct sources.
9. ___ My paragraphs are in order.
10. ___ My introduction grabs the reader's attention.
11. ___ My work has a quality conclusion.

12. ___ My paper is written neatly, so it can be read easily.

13. ___ My work is written in my own words.

I can't understand how anyone can write without rewriting anything over and over again. I scarcely ever re-read my published writings, but if by chance I come across a page, it always strikes me: "all this must be rewritten; this is how I should have written it. . . ."

—Leo Tolstoy

STEP 4. TUNING IT UP: EDITING

The editing step in the writing process provides time for the author to correct spelling, punctuation, capitalization, grammar, and the overall appearance of the selection. The student works individually, with a partner, or in a small group. Remind the author to take the writing, the revisions, and a pencil to meet with his editor. The author reads his writing. The editing goal is for the author to improve the work by using the suggestions of others as a step to learning how to self-edit.

Teacher's Role for the Editing Step

The teacher models his thinking and reasoning by explaining each procedure in the editing process. As the steps are introduced sequentially and thoroughly, students learn the "how to's" of editing.

Give students the opportunity to edit their own work. Allow time for the students to work on their papers at the beginning of the editing stage. For example, they need to locate each misspelled word, circle it, look it up, and write the correct spelling above it.

Avoid red marks and negative comments. Let students mark errors on their paper. Give them specific rules and guidelines. This is a learning process. Young authors learn through self-corrections. Remind students that everyone learns from mistakes.

Plan partner or small group conferences for editing. In a conference, the audience offers suggestions as the author makes desired corrections. For example, the group may check correct use of punctuation marks at the end of each sentence. This "punctuation talk" is an excellent way for students to share and learn writing skills.

Mechanic Antics

The mechanics of writing are the signs and symbols, such as punctuation and capitalization, placed in the author's writing. The signs and symbols guide the readers' understanding of the author's expressions and meaning. The placement of these signals often becomes a barrier to good writing when they are overemphasized. Used appropriately, however, these writing tools make the author's thoughts clear, so the audience will understand his ideas.

1. Sentence Sense

Each sentence must express a complete thought. Look for fragments and correct them. Be sure each sentence has a subject and verb.

2. Grammar Gab

The following Fix It Solutions are included in the Editing step of the writing process because it involves choosing the tense, the nouns with the appropriate verbs, and the pronouns. Authors often recognize grammar errors when they read their own work orally. Some common grammar rules for students to use in editing follow:

1. Sequence of tenses

   a. Wrong: He plays ball, studies his homework, and needed to go to work.

   b. Correct: He plays ball, studies his homework, and needs to go to work.

2. Noun agreement

   a. Wrong: Jim and Jacob looks at the cows.

   b. Correct: Jim and Jacob look at the cows.

3. Pronoun reference

   a. Wrong: The student works on the writing and then they meet with a partner to share the work.

   b. Correct: The student works on the writing and then he meets with a partner to share the work.

3. Capitalization

Use a capital letter for

- The first word in a sentence
- Names of people and special places

- Names for days of the week, month, and holidays
- Commercial products
- Names of organizations and groups
- Titles of books, movies, songs, poems, and articles
- Headings and subheadings

4. Sentence Stop Signs

Use a period, question mark, or exclamation point correctly at the end of sentences.

5. Comma Cues

Commas make the author's thoughts easy to read and understand. Here are some of the most common comma rules:

Use commas

- To separate the day and year in a date
- Between the city and state in an address
- Between two complete thoughts in a sentence that are connected with the words such as *and, but, for, or, nor, so,* or *yet*
- On both sides of a proper noun when used in the middle of a sentence
- After the greeting and closing comments in a letter
- Between words in a sequence
- To set off words in an introduction. Example: First, _____ _____

6. Colons: Dot Duo

A colon is used before a list and before a long quotation in a passage.

7. Quotation Quotes

Use quotation marks to show what a person is saying. The marks go before and after a direct quote. Remember, it is not necessary to use quotation marks in a speech bubble when drawing cartoons. A speech bubble indicates that the individual near the bubble is talking.

Spelling Corrections

Ask the author to read his own work, so he can find his spelling errors. Tell him to circle words spelled incorrectly and correct them on the Sloppy Copy. Encourage the author to use all available resources, such as a dictionary, thesaurus, textbook, or word bank. Encourage him to use his favorite Cool Tools. Partners can work together to find the correct spelling.

Developing Spellers

The student needs to work and/or play with a word he cannot spell. Use the students' intelligence strengths and learning styles in the activity to teach him the correct spelling of a word. For instance, if the student's strong areas of intelligence are art and music, encourage him to write the word in graffiti ways or incorporate the word in a drawing. Give him opportunities to use the word in a rap, rhyme, jingle, or song. If he enjoys working with others, assign a peer tutor or assistant to participate in his spelling practice sessions, games, and activities.

A student may approach spelling in his own way. Encourage the student to use the approach that works best. The following list is a sample of the many ways a student may learn to spell. (See the section on invented spelling.)

Say the word and spell it.

- Use the sounds in each syllable.
- Think about word families and rhyming words that have the same sounds.
- Categorize the word with similar words and memorize the list. Look at the word's shape or configuration.
- Find the root or base word.
- Identify the prefix and/or suffix.

Provide opportunities for the student to practice spelling words in varied ways. Practice the spelling of a word until the student takes ownership of the word by spelling it automatically. Assess the writer's spelling ability by identifying the words he has mastered or spelled correctly.

Making Repairs

Use writing samples with repetitions, omitted words, or incorrect spelling to demonstrate ways to correct mechanical errors. Provide the student with shortcuts to correct errors such as cutting and pasting, drawing lines through them, and marking each one with an arrow. Use these activities when the student works alone, with a partner, with groups, or with the total class.

Out With the Old, In With the New: Writing Habits

Habits are hard to break. Students must have a strong desire or "buy-in" to break a writing habit. They must be convinced that the new skill or strategy is better than the one they currently use.

Identify bad writing habits to make the author aware of specific problems. Modeling is an excellent way to demonstrate correct writing. It takes time, practice, and patience to change bad writing habits.

Habits to Break

- **Uses too many words to express thoughts**

  Do not say the same thing twice. Identify words that are unnecessary. If you need to explain or repeat something, use different words.
- **Uses too few words**

  Use enough words to make your points and create understanding.
- **Uses "big words"**

  Big words are not always the best choice.

  Use the best words, not necessarily the big words.
- **Uses too many "I" words**

  Use the word *you* more than *I*.
- **Writes unnecessary information**

  Write about topics or subjects that interest or are needed by readers.

  Remember, "If the information is interesting or needed, they will read it!"

Figure 4.4   Mechanical Check-Up

Student _____ Date _____ Title _____

Skills	Yes	No	Comments
1. I started each sentence with a capital letter.		No	3rd line
2. I capitalized the names of people.			
3. I began names of special places and things with a capital letter.			
4. I used the correct punctuation at the end of my sentences.			
5. I corrected misspelled words.			
6. Someone read my work to be sure it made sense.			
7. I used quotation marks for dialogue.			
8. I indented paragraphs.			
9. My words are spaced for easy reading.			
Others			

STEP 5. NEAT SHEET: FINAL COPY

After the Editing step is complete, the work is ready to become a Neat Sheet. The author uses his Sloppy Copy with the revision and editing notes to make the final copy. Design each final-draft experience as an exciting, rewarding event to give the author a feeling of accomplishment and pride. Remind the student that he has taken the writing from his original thoughts through the steps of the writing process to produce his masterpiece. Remember, the goal for the Neat Sheet is improvement, not perfection. The final copy may contain errors, but it reflects the author's best work at this time.

There are many steps that take an author's work from the prewriting to the final copy in the writing process. In most assignments the student needs to work through the Sloppy Copy step. Very few writing assignments need to become Neat Sheets.

Teacher's Role in the Final Copy

Model appearance expectations for the final copy. Show tips and techniques for indenting, spacing, neatness, and legible writing. The student needs to know how to format his work in various forms. Remember, most genres use different formats. Share various formatting examples, so the student may adapt the ideas in his writing. Refer to the writer as the "artist at work." Tell the author that his goal for the final copy is to produce his "best work" or masterpiece.

Provide the time, space, and materials to write the Neat Sheet. Consider individual needs for this step. Remember, a student may need extra time.

Let the student choose the Write Spot where he can work alone and concentrate. Remind the author to use his revision and editing notes with his Sloppy Copy to develop the final edition.

Provide quality writing implements and the appropriate paper for the authors. If a computer with writing software is available, allow the student to compose his final copy using a word processing program. *Remember, the goal is to improve writing, not to perfect it.* Compare the student's Prewriting, Sloppy Copy, and final copy. Look for improvements. Assess strengths and weaknesses. The writer's growth in the experiences will be evident. Identify skills to teach or reinforce in future writing experiences.

STEP 6. PUBLISHING:
SHARING AND CELEBRATING

In the Publishing step of the writing process, the author shares the writing with classmates or special guests. This may involve a formal or informal viewing of the work. Choose writing selections to place in a notebook, display on walls, post on the Web, or place in the student's portfolio. The publication is a presentation of the author's "best work" for a specific stage of writing. It is a time to celebrate!

Teacher's Role in the Publishing Step

Provide time for the student to share his writing. Allow the reading of the selection with partners, small groups, and total class. Invite an audience for the celebration, such as other classes, administrators, or honored guests. The author needs to rehearse the reading before sharing with an audience. Watch the writer's confidence grow through these experiences.

Display the author's work. The student's work creates a print-rich environment related to the lesson. The writing samples make excellent bulletin board, wall, door, and hall displays. Take advantage of publishing opportunities for the young author in magazines, Web sites, newspapers, contests, and community displays.

Plan reflection periods for students to process the experience. Students need to reflect on their writing experiences in a journal. Encourage authors to think about the skills and strategies they learn along the way. The journal provides opportunities for the authors to express and analyze their feelings about writing experiences. Each successful accomplishment creates positive attitudes toward the activities. If the reflection is negative, make changes. The information gained from reflection activities benefits the student and the teacher.

Be an active listener as the author reads. Give specific feedback for the selection read, so the author realizes the value of having a good listener. If appropriate, provide the audience opportunities to enter the feedback discussion.

Express interest and enthusiasm for the publication. Let students hear sincere, specific praise for their writing. Positive oral and written comments motivate writers. Praise, praise, praise! Praise the work to teachers, staff members, and parents in the student's presence. This recognition inspires and rewards young authors.

Publishing Debuts

Try some of the following suggestions to celebrate the authors' work and growth as a writer. Ask students for more celebration ideas.

Authors' Reception

- Invite parents, grandparents, and special friends.
- Have a selection or book signing.
- Provide a cake decorated with a large book, balloons, and confetti.
- Display the written masterpieces.
- Make banners to reflect words of celebration and congratulations.
- Ask the young authors to dress for the occasion.
- Designate an author's chair. (See Author's Chair following for guidelines.)
- Have someone introduce the author.
- Record or videotape the author as he reads.
- Present a copy of the writing to a special guest to honor him.

Author's Chair

Use the Author's Chair as a special event in the classroom or with invited guests.

1. Rehearse the first reading with partners or small groups to work out pauses, expressions, and mechanics.

2. Send an invitation to another class, parents, and special guests.

3. The author reads from a special chair designated as "The Author's Chair." Place a reading lamp nearby. Use a podium and a microphone to make the event a more formal affair.

4. Have the author sign copies of his work.

Designate an author's chair for students to use each time they share writing with the total class.

MORE PUBLISHING IDEAS

- Create a video of the reading.
- Make a Big Book or a Mini Book.
- Record the reading so others may listen to it. Use a unique sound before a page is turned.
- Add copies of the books to the class or school library.
- Enter writing selections in local, district, state, national, and international contests.
- Submit the writing to magazines for publication.

DISPLAY PLACES AND SPACES

Doors	Hallways	Parent letters	Flyers	Bulletin boards
Newspapers	Web sites	Store windows	Magazines	
Clotheslines		Handmade books	Walls	

AUTHOR'S REFLECTIONS

Think about the steps in the writing process and check the items you completed well.

Author _____ Date _____ Title _____

1. ___ I brainstormed ideas.

2. ___ I discussed my ideas with a classmate.

3. ___ I used my time wisely to gather information.

4. ___ The details supported the main idea.

5. ___ The story was told in sequence.

6. ___ I included graphics in my writing. (*if needed*)

7. ___ I read my work aloud to someone.

8. ___ I revised my work.

9. ___ I corrected mechanics: punctuation, capitalization, and spelling.

10. ___ I am ready to publish my work.

Complete the following:

1. The hardest part of the writing experience was _____.

2. The easiest part of the writing experience was _____.

3. I still need to work on _____.

4. I improved my writing by _____.

Comments

_____

5

Instructional Strategies and Activities for the Differentiated Writing Classroom

The migratory patterns of butterflies are innate.
Learning strategies become internalized guides for authors.

DIFFERENTIATING WRITING STYLES AND GENRES

Genres intrigue and motivate students. In her book *In the Middle: New Understandings About Writing, Reading, and Learning* (1998), Nancie Atwell emphasizes the value of writers using genres to express themselves. By varying genres, students learn different ways to communicate through writing. The teacher who challenges students to use various writing forms and genres to learn, report, and process information can take the "same old way" or the ruts out of teaching in the content areas.

Genres provide students with exciting, novel ways to think about content information. Facts, concepts, and ideas applied in a unique writing format will be remembered because each genre presents a different way to record and retain the information learned. The following list of genres contains a brief explanation of each one. Challenge students to add more genres to the list.

Advertisements, Theme Songs, and Jingles

The advertising world uses commercials with theme songs and jingles to make us remember their products. Use these tools to enhance learners' memory of details and facts. Students enjoy using these creative ways to remember topic information.

Autobiography

An autobiography is a story or book an individual writes about his or her own life. When a student writes a story about his life, the writing becomes a personalized experience. A personal survey can be used to gather data for an autobiography. An autobiography can be adapted to nonliving things by using personification. Nonliving things come alive when they take on the characteristics of human beings.

Biography

A biography is a story or book an individual writes about another person's life. The information for the story or book usually comes from extended research or interviews.

Book Review

A book review presents the author's opinion on a book he has read. The key points, the highlights, and the best and worst features of the book are disclosed.

Calendars and Day Planners

Calendars and day planners are used every day. They record schedules and appointments, To Do lists, phone numbers, and personal goals. Students may keep calendars or logs to post school events, important things to remember, and assignments.

Cartoons and Comic Strips

Use the humor of cartoons and comic strips to make mundane information and concepts come alive. Humor enhances learning, relieves stress, and reduces tension in life for individuals of all ages. Ask students to create comic strips or cartoons using the information in their unit of study. Artistic talents will be tapped as the characters and scenes are developed. Place the characters' conversations in speech bubbles to elicit the students' interpretation of emotions and feelings. The scenes will reflect the learners' understanding of the information.

Cartoons and comic strips are effective tools to use to compare and contrast new facts, to show humor in situations, and to illustrate fact and opinion. Try editorial cartoons to teach skills with a point of view. The creation of each frame will show what the student knows, his interpretation, and his understanding. Written assignments using cartoons and comic strips are popular because students enjoy connecting humor and learning.

Dialogue

Ask the student to write and role-play the conversations of characters. The dialogue will reflect the student's interpretations of facts, personalities, and emotions. Record the character's words in various situations and time periods. Assign the role of inventor, botanist, astronaut, hero, archeologist, historian, family member, friend, mathematician, artist, actor, or other individual in the unit of focus.

Remember that objects or living things may be personified using dialogue. For example, record an opal conversing with an emerald or a tree in the rain forest chatting with a tree in the desert.

E-mail

E-mail is a popular communicating tool used by students. In classroom experiences, e-mail may be used for tutoring, homework, notes, interviews, or research. This technology is used in almost every home and business and will grow in popularity. E-mail gives students experiences they enjoy while preparing them for tomorrow's world.

Experience Charts

Write the student's discussion notes, lists, and stories on a chart or transparency using the student's words as they are expressed. This is an effective way to model writing and work with student responses.

Lists

Lists may be used to alphabetize, categorize, chunk, sequence, and sort information. The items are placed in memory by jotting them down. Most lists are created to assist memory. Information in a list is easier to recall than words or phrases in paragraph form. These organizational tools are quick and easy to remember. Grocery needs are placed on lists. Many individuals make "To Do" lists and check off each item as it is completed. Some people make mental notes from the lists and use them to accomplish the tasks. A student uses his random, brainstormed lists to categorize and sort information.

Magazine Articles

Writing an article for a favorite magazine is an effective activity because it gives the student a chance to write on a topic of interest. If possible, encourage the student to choose the magazine. Teacher and parent approval may be required if magazines are brought from home. The article does not have to be submitted for the student to meet a writing goal and enjoy the experience.

Photo Essays

Write a detailed report about an individual or a group of people, an event, concept, or discovery in picture form. The pictures may have captions or dialogue to provide more information. A picture is worth a thousand words. The pictures may be photographs, cut-out pictures or drawings, or a combination. Photos may be used to illustrate a procedure or directions. It is fun to assign photo essays as follow-up activities for a special study or a field trip.

Predictions

Predictions are guesses about what will happen next. Write predictions for experiments, text passages, or events. The guesses foster thinking and intrigue the student to see if his predictions were correct. Honor all guesses and have discussions about reasons the predictions or ideas will or will not work. Prediction skills are used in the thinking classroom.

Profiles

Profiles are detailed reports or outlines of an event or incident. They may describe an individual or a group of people. Profiles may include the highlights of a person's life or give a detailed description of an event. They provide an accurate account and a novel way of writing a report.

Sitcoms

Students are interested in television sitcoms, so use these programs to spark writing ideas. For instance, students may take notes and identify the main idea and supporting details in their favorite episode. This is an excellent comprehension activity. Students may need parent approval to watch the sitcom.

USING PERSONIFICATION TO PROCESS CONTENT INFORMATION

Personification gives physical abilities, behaviors, and other characteristics of human beings to plants, animals, and nonliving things. The student will eagerly apply personification to process content information.

Example 1: The Trail of Tears

- Subject: History
- Topic: The Trail of Tears
- Genre: Historical Fiction

The road remembered the shuffle of moccasins and the teardrops that fell. She knew the Cherokee Indians were being herded on a long, forced, walking journey from their homes in the East to their new reservations in the West. The road could hear the sadness in the Indian voices. She could hear the cries of babies as they bounced along on the backs of their weary mothers. The road knew why she would always be remembered as the Trail of Tears.

Example 2: Cule E. Mol Goes Underground

- Subject: Science
- Topic: Diffusion
- Genre: Mystery
- Vocabulary bonus: The name *Cule E. Mol* was created from scrambling the syllables in *molecule*, a vocabulary word.

His name is Cule E. Mol. He is a water molecule. He is on the FBI's Most Wanted List. Cule E. Mol was last seen condensing with his friends as they came to Earth disguised as a raindrop.

It is believed that they went underground and entered the root of a tree with a group of his molecule cohorts. They were traced moving through the root. They diffused to travel separately through the stems and leaves. The large plant will be indicted for using osmosis to harbor the fugitives.

The FBI plans to take Cule E. Mol into custody before he evaporates and escapes. If he is not captured, he is expected to travel on wind currents to another continent and condense there. He may be camouflaged on an ice cap, flow with the current of a great river, or continue his condensing and evaporating escapades.

FANTASTIC FORMATS AND GENRES GALORE

Adventures

Advertisements

Announcements

Autobiographies

Billboards

Biographies

Book jackets

Book reports

Books

Brochures

Bumper stickers

Categories

Comedies

Comic strips

Commercials

Contracts

Critiques

Debates

Definitions

Diaries

Directions

Editorials

E-mail messages

Epitaphs

Essays

Fables

Fantasies

Faxes

Ghost stories

Graffiti

Grocery lists

Guidelines

Handbooks

Historical fiction

Interviews

Jingles

Journals

Labels

Letters

Lists

Logos

Magazine articles

Memoirs

Memos

Mysteries

Myths

Newspaper articles

Observation notes

Parodies

Plays

Poems

Position statements

Protest signs

Puzzles

Questionnaires

Quotes

Recipes

Reminders

Reports

Responses

Reviews

Riddles

Rules

Sagas

Satires

Scenarios

Scripts

Signs

Sketches

Song lyrics

Speeches

Sport stories

Sports events

Spy tales

Stories

Summaries

Suspense stories

Tall tales

Task directions

Thrillers

Tongue twisters

Travelogues

War stories

Westerns

Wills

Words of wisdom

TEACHING WRITING STRATEGIES

Teachers know that a learning strategy is a procedure used to learn and apply new information. Students need time to encode important information, to connect it to prior knowledge, and to practice using it in problem solving (Siegler, 1998). So, too, a young author must learn how to use each writing strategy thoroughly, so that he will be able to apply it automatically as needed.

Teach Each Writing Strategy Strategically

Students must be taught how and when to use different writing *strategies*. A writing strategy must be taught *strategically* and *explicitly*. The teacher models each step by verbally explaining and demonstrating the thinking that accompanies it. When students hear the teacher's thinking, they learn how to organize their own thoughts as they work with a writing strategy. Each practice session is guided and monitored until the students apply the strategy automatically. When the students master the skill, their oral thinking becomes self-talk.

LANGUAGE EXPERIENCE ACTIVITIES

In a Language Experience activity, the teacher writes a student's exact words, "word for word." The teacher records the statements of one or more students as they contribute their thoughts to form a list, a discussion, or a story. Each student observes his words as they are recorded.

Language Experiences demonstrate the writing and reading connection. The learner observes the letters forming words, the words making sentences, and sentences creating paragraphs as the words are written on a chart. The Language Experience is a vital tool because a student can read his own words in writing. He may need guidance while reading. The Language Experience is effective with individuals, small groups, or a total class.

Students gather near the teacher so they can see the words as they are written. It is very important for students to see the chart, board, paper, or computer screen where their words are recorded. Chart paper is easy to handle and move. It can be displayed and revisited as needed.

The teacher repeats each student's words as they are written. This models how the spoken word becomes written. Students may not understand that what they say is written on the paper. Let them know, This is writing! Learners may know the words they want to say, but they cannot write them. Language Experience activities train students to write the words as they say them.

Language Experience for the Emergent Learner

The teacher usually selects the topic for the Language Experience. The class may choose a title before the writing begins. A catchy, clever title may be chosen at the end of the story.

Students give the information to the teacher orally by telling it. The teacher writes the sentence, saying the name of each letter as it is formed. The teacher names the letter as it is written. The students repeat the name of the letter. For example, if a student's sentence began with the letter *T*, the teacher says "Capital *T*." The student repeats it, saying, "Capital *T*." When the letters have formed a word, the teacher and the student say the word together. For example, he says, "Capital *T-h-e* spells *The*." Using this method, the teacher reinforces the name of each letter, recognition of every word, and connecting words to make a sentence. When a sentence is complete, the teacher reads the sentence while the students listen. Students repeat the sentence. The teacher uses a pointer to identify each word as it is read.

As learners become more proficient with letter recognition, spelling, and reading, their progress is evident. Students' voices join the teacher's voice as they say the letters and words when they are written.

When a chart is complete, the students and the teacher read the entire story, passage, or list. The teacher may need to read one sentence at a time and ask the students to repeat it. The experience ends with the oral reading. The students need to read and hear the words on the chart to gain an understanding of the writing and reading connection.

The same process is used when a student in the early stages of writing composes a journal story. The student needs someone to write his story as he says the words.

Language Experience in the Upper Grades

Language Experience activities are effective in the upper grades. If the teacher records the words of a student, it is a Language Experience. For example, this procedure is used on the board, overhead, or computer projection screen to record student responses during a small group or class discussion.

When the teacher uses this procedure, he models the thinking skills needed to answer questions related to the reading or the discussion. The teacher demonstrates his thinking step by step. For example, a student realizes that as he speaks, the teacher is scripting his words. When a learner needs to respond to an open-ended question on a test, he realizes that the words he is thinking should be written. As the words are said orally, the student learns to write them down. Teachers say students often know answers but cannot transfer the information to test forms. The Language Experience activity develops metacognitive writing skills.

Figure 5.1   Language Experience Charts: Adjustable Assignment

	High Degree of Mastery	Approaching Mastery	Beginning Mastery
B	• View his story in print. • Increase his sight-reading vocabulary. • Needs to transfer this skill to note taking.	• Develop an understanding of word-to-sentence construction • Add to his word-mastery list • Needs to see his spoken words in print	• More opportunities to see words in print • Follow words in print as the information is read aloud • Needs to see words written and spelled as they are spoken • Develop a letter-to-word connection
A	• Writes and reads the story as a leading contributor to the Language Experience process • Has a strong knowledge base of language and sentence construction • Usually spells the word before the teacher writes the word • Is a fluent, comprehending reader	• Contributes to the story or topic • Recognizes and knows how to spell most common words • Reads many words without assistance	• Can repeat letters and words after the teacher • Reads a few words without assistance

Key: A. What does this group know now?
        B. What does this group need to know next?

The chart in Figure 5.1 lists skills and suggests assignments for students at different levels of mastery.

Use Probing Questions

A big mistake teachers make as they record students' statements is to misinterpret the statements. The teacher should always ask for clarification. If the teacher writes misinterpreted information, the student may not volunteer to correct the teacher. Encourage the student to give further explanations. If the information is not clear, ask the student probing questions or make encouraging statements. For example, say, "Tell me more." Probing statements and questions will elicit explanations that usually clarify the previous statement. Create a risk-free environment so each student feels free to express himself. Let the student know that in this class it is important for everyone to know and understand all statements. Clear communication lines are vital to productive work with Language Experience activities. Here are examples of probing questions and statements:

Tell me more.

What part do you not understand?

Explain this _____.

What does _____ mean?

Record the student's words on the chart, overhead, board, computer, or paper. Identify the key words from what the student says. Spell the important vocabulary words as they are written. Say the word after all the letters in the word are written. The student spells and says the words with the teacher. The repetition reinforces word recognition and correct spelling of words.

BRAINSTORMING

For me the initial delight is in the surprise of remembering something I didn't know I knew.

—Robert Frost

Brainstorming involves recording each thought that comes to mind when a word or topic is presented. This thinking strategy teaches the student to bring his thoughts and ideas out of memory storage. As ideas are expressed, each one is listed so it can be considered for use in the writing assignment. The techniques used in brainstorming are selected to trigger visual images, sounds, words, and feelings.

Use brainstorming to understand a student's prior experiences with the topic. Related information the student has seen, heard, or read is recalled through visual imagery, the senses, and feelings. For example, if a student recalls a ride at the fair as a pleasant experience, excitement will be evident. If the experience was unpleasant, fear is expressed.

Brainstorming activities may involve the class, a group, or individuals. Remember this handy tip! Give students a quiet time to list their thoughts independently before they brainstorm with small or large groups. The student's individual list makes it easier for him to contribute to the group's brainstorming session. (See Idea Round-Up in Prewriting section of Chapter 4.)

Mental Shopping

My brain has more space than any store.
Its shelves make room for thoughts galore!
I can shop for facts and ideas on the shelves of my mind.
The information I have stored is easy to find.

— Chapman & King, 2003

Brainstorming Guidelines

The following guidelines make a brainstorming activity a success in any classroom.

- Work in small groups.
- Assign a recorder to list the ideas.
- Brainstorm a list on the assigned or chosen topic.
- Encourage "piggy-backing" on ideas.
- Accept each response.
- Ask teams to select the top ten or *best* responses.
- Categorize or group items on the lists to link details and create order.
- Cluster thoughts by plotting them on a graphic organizer.
- Create a class list as items are discussed.

PROMPTS TO "JUMP START" THINKING

Prompts are statements or questions that focus the students' attention on a topic and stimulate or "jump start" their thinking. Often prompts provide ideas for writing experiences. If students work in pairs or groups to respond to the prompts, they may produce one paper. If one response sheet is required, each student may need a copy of the work for his journal or portfolio.

Vary the format for required responses. For example, the student may use symbols, pictures, actions, words, or numbers as answers.

"Jump Start" Prompts

1. How did you find the answer?

2. How do _____ and _____ compare or contrast?

3. Write the steps you used to solve this problem.

4. What was the easiest part of this problem?

5. What does _____ mean to you?

6. What were you thinking as you worked this problem?

7. Write the directions to _____ *(games, activities, procedures)*

8. I would choose _____ as the answer because _____.

9. Would you use _____'s way of solving the problem or _____'s way? Why?

> *Words just float here and there in my mind*
> *When I search for them, they're easy to find.*
>
> —Chapman & King, 2003

JOURNALING

Journaling is a way for a person to write freely in order to place thoughts, feelings, and ideas on paper. Often writing is a form of therapy. This form of writing gives an individual the opportunity to express privately what is on his mind. Journaling is designed as an exciting addition to most units of study. Remember, the more an individual writes, the more he perfects his skills. Journaling is an effective way to incorporate meaningful writing practice in daily activities. Following are some of the most useful journal formats for processing and recording information in the content areas.

Photo Scrapbook Journals

Use photos, pictures from magazines, or pictures drawn by the students to illustrate the thoughts, ideas, reflections, and facts learned. The student explains the visuals with captions that link to the information studied. This activity brings information alive in picture form, and the captions give the student writing practice with text.

Comic Journals

Comic journals contain cartoons to illustrate the happenings, characters, and facts in the unit. Humor combined with art is an exciting way to interpret and retain information. The captions may add humor to the content. This activity may be used to record opinions in editorial cartoons.

Content Journals

Content journals are used to record information learned about topics through reading, hands-on experiences, videos, demonstrations, projects, field trips, research, and other sources.

"What Are You Thinking?" Journals

Use "What Are You Thinking?" journals for a student to reflect on the step-by-step processes of his thinking. For example, the journal may be in the form of a training manual with steps to assemble a product or outline the procedures to solve a problem. Illustrations and explanations may be included. In math classrooms, the metacognitive journal may sequence steps for solving a problem. During a science lesson, a student may follow the process used as an experiment. This activity may be used with a hands-on project. The author explains his "self-talk" or thinking while completing the project.

EQ (Emotional Quotient) Journals

In an EQ journal, the student records his feelings and emotions during a unit of study, an experience, or an assignment. The date, time, place, and experience are noted as part of each journal entry. Key starters for EQ journal entries are

- The color of today's events is _____ because _____.
- I like _____. I dislike _____.
- When I _____ I feel like a _____ because _____.
- The theme song for this lesson would be _____.
- My *aha!* is _____.

Log Journals

Log journals record the events of a project, a study, an adventure, or a discovery. Include the date when the things are explored, seen, and learned. Personal insights, reflections, hypotheses, and thoughts are a crucial part of the log experience.

Partner Journals

Partner journals use paper divided in two equal parts. One student writes a journal entry on one side of the paper. His partner writes back on the opposite side, making comments on the topics addressed. In most cases, the student chooses his partner. He usually chooses someone he trusts so he can share ideas, questions, and thoughts freely.

EXAMPLE

Date/Student's Entry | Date/Partner's Response

Note Journals

Note journals use paper divided in two equal parts. The student writes notes from the study of a section of information on the left-hand side of the page while it is read or discussed. When reviewing the same material, he makes additions and corrections to the notes on the right-hand side.

More Journaling Formats and Activities

Here are additional suggestions for varying journal formats to complement special assignments, units, topics, or projects:

Dear Diary journal	Survey journal	Data Collection journal
Observation journal	Journalist journal	I SPY journal
Another Voice journal	Homework log	Technical journal
Scientific journal	Math log	Learning journal
Roving Reporter notes	Response journal	Interview journal
Personal journal		

Write On

Allow students the opportunity to use a variety of writing supplies for journaling. Vary materials with the assignments. Add to the following suggestions. Make journaling an exciting, rewarding, learning experience for students. Make them want to say, "Look at my journal!"

Spiral notebook	Loose-leaf notebook	Personalized folder
Clipboard	Day calendar	Shape book
Computer disc	Note pad	Scroll
Legal pad	Diary	

Create your own "Write On" journal

Teacher's Role in Journaling

Choose the journaling genre, type, shape, and size to fit the assignment and the expectations. Remember to make the experience novel and interesting, so the activities are intriguing for the student. Vary the writing forms. Think what it would be like to complete assignments and activities in the same way in every class. Make the assignments appeal to the learner, so he wants to accomplish the mission and learn.

Set expectations and guidelines. If students are expected to meet specific criteria in their journal activities, make expectations concise and clear.

Foster creativity and expression. Encourage students to express their emotions and feelings in their own way. Assign opportunities that promote "thinking outside the box" and higher-order thinking skills. Accept and honor students' ideas.

Allow time. Remember, it takes time to think! One learner may like to journal more than other students. One student may know more information than others about the topic; therefore he needs more time to write. Interest levels vary. When an interest level is high, and curiosity is stirred, the author needs more time to write.

GATHERING RESEARCH

Research involves discovering or finding as much related information as possible about a topic. The important information is organized and recorded. Topics for research are chosen from the unit of study. They are usually selected and assigned by the teacher. Teach students how to strategically and purposefully conduct research. Model the research strategy that matches the assignment.

Contracts and Proposals for Research

Contracts give the students opportunities to choose the tools and methods they will use to complete their research. This is an excellent way to differentiate an assignment.

Consider providing a list of topics from which each student will choose a research interest area. Give the student a contract or agreement that specifies how the research will be conducted and reported.

Contract Agreements

The teacher or the student writes a contract agreement. The contract form outlines the work to accomplish, the timeline for completion, general requirements, the sources, and procedures. Here is a suggested contract form:

Contract Agreement

Name _____   Teacher _____   Date _____

Topic _____   Subject _____

I agree to use the following sources: _____ _____ _____.

The criteria for the assignment are _____ _____ _____.

The format for the report will be _____.

The length of the report is a maximum of _____ pages.

The work is to be completed by _____. *(date)*

Student signature _____

Teacher signature_____

Contract Proposals

Occasionally, a student may not find a topic of interest on the list. Permit him or her to submit another area of interest for approval on a contract proposal. Keep in mind that the student's proposed topic must fit the unit of study and meet the assignment's criteria. If the majority of the class has an assigned topic, make the same requirements for the class and the student who is submitting an individual contract. This minimizes the time needed to assess the work.

A contract proposal is a form submitted with the student's plans for the research assignment. The proposal permits the student to design the agreement. The learner submits the topic, the sources he plans to use, the procedures for completing it, and how the information is presented. The contract proposal must receive teacher approval. The student may need advice and guidance.

Contract Proposal Form

Dear _____ (Teacher's name)

I would like to write a research report on _____.

I am interested in learning:

a. _____   b. _____   c. _____.

I plan to gather information from _____, _____, and _____.

I plan to write my report in the following form:

___ Interview ___ Skit ___ Book

___ Poster ___ Charts ___ Multimedia ___ Booklet

Student's Signature _____   Date_____

Sample Contract Proposal: *Online Surfing* (Researching the Web)

Name _____   Date _____

Topic _____

Subtopics _____ _____

My search engine will be _____

I plan to surf the following sites:

_____ _____ _____ _____

General Research Guidelines

1. Tell why you are conducting the research.

2. Identify your sources or places where you found the information.

3. Gather all the information and data.

4. Separate facts from views and opinions.

5. Select the most important facts.

6. Delete unnecessary facts and ideas.

7. Organize the information.

8. Write the research results in your own words.

Ways to Research a Topic

- Brainstorm
- Discuss
- Interview
- Listen
- Read
- Surf the Web
- View a movie clip

Presenting Research Reports with "Zippidy-Do"

Provide time and materials for the learners to give informative, creative presentations related to their research. Provide opportunities for students to prepare reports using the information in unique ways.

Most research reports are perceived as boring and stressful. However, conducting and reporting research can be powerful tools for learning. The student becomes an expert with his topic. Do not miss valuable teaching moments when the learner's interest and enthusiasm is high! Differentiate research reports using these novel suggestions:

- Create diagrams and charts.
- Use caricatures.
- Illustrate with a poster.
- Develop a game.
- Create a skit.
- Write a play.
- Develop a video presentation.
- Design a galley display.
- Create a computer presentation.
- Record a radio skit.
- Design a Web page.

Research Conferences

Schedule conference checkpoints periodically during the research process. These meetings are conducted with partners, small groups, or the teacher. A student feels accountable and takes more responsibility if he knows he will talk about the information. Conference preparations give the learner a sense of ownership in his work.

The following form may guide the research conference:

Name _____ Date _____ Teacher _____

Topic _____ Subject _____

My sources were _____ _____ _____.

Here is an overview of my research. _____.

I have completed _____.

I need to work on _____.

My work will be presented in the form of _____
(an essay, a speech, a report).

I will present my research to _____.

Figure 5.2 recommends assignments for students with different levels of mastery of research skills.

Teacher's Role in Research

- Present standards and expectations.
- Model step-by-step procedures.
- Provide topic choices.
- Give specific guidelines.
- Provide a checklist.
- Provide an assessment rubric.
- Monitor preset dates throughout the project.
- Provide conference time and feedback.
- Permit the student to choose his presentation form.

NOTE TAKING

Notes assist recall of facts and ideas gathered from reading or listening. As notes are recorded, the brain focuses attention and processes the information. A student may not know how to take notes. He must be taught this skill.

Note-Taking Tips for Listening

GET READY

- Have a favorite writing implement and paper ready.
- Use your favorite note-taking tools, such as a highlighter and sticky notes.
- Choose a seat that makes the speaker and his materials visible.
- Check the area to avoid anything that interferes with hearing.
- Review previous information in notes, handouts, or the text.

Figure 5.2 Adjustable Model for Research

	High Degree of Mastery	Approaching Mastery	Beginning
B	• Research opportunities of choice • Independent time assigned to explore resource materials and gathering data • Work through approved contracts • Learn how to apply information in a wide variety of reference materials	• Needs more opportunities to research • Needs feedback at each step of the procedure	• Works slowly and strategically through each step of the research procedure • Needs feedback on progress • Needs a strong prewriting organizer • Needs to read first draft aloud • Needs to learn how to use references • Needs to learn how to use the assistance of a peer or an adult
A	• Uses a variety of materials as resources • Defines and expands topic clearly • Works independently and productively • Reflects creativity • Applies accurate information	• Uses two or more sources to locate information • Stays on topic • Needs little assistance • Is aware of purpose • Organizes information and materials	• Uses one source for given topic • Wanders from the topic • Requires ongoing assistance • Lacks awareness of purpose • Uses poor organization skills

Standard: To be an effective researcher
Key: A. What do they know now?
   B. What do they need to learn next?

GET SET

- Turn off other thoughts.
- Focus on the speaker's words.
- Anticipate what will be said.

GO

- Be mentally at the starting line and ready when the speaker begins.
- Record key points in your own words.

- Use organizers such as lists, outlines, webs, and timelines with your notes.
- Ask yourself questions similar to the following:

EXAMPLES

How will I use this information?
What is the best way to record the information to remember it?

- Make notes on information that is repeated for emphasis.
- Listen for signals that tell you valuable information is coming. These word and phrase cues include:

EXAMPLES

Again I would like to point out _____.
The key is to _____.
The steps are _____.
In summary, _____.

Note-Taking Tips for Reading

As books and materials are read in the information search, it is important to pay attention to the most valuable data and ideas. The following guidelines are useful when taking notes from reading.

PREPARE

- Have a favorite writing implement and paper ready.
- Use your most effective tools, such as a highlighter and sticky notes.
- Choose a comfortable place to read.
- Check the area to avoid anything that interferes with reading.

FOCUS

- Turn off other thoughts.
- Concentrate on the reading material.
- Review previous chapters or notes.
- Preview the headings and subtitles.

WRITE

- Write important information and ideas in your own words.
- Use key words, phrases, or lists.
- Place the information on a graphic organizer, if needed.

- Highlight important facts and details.
- Circle, box, or highlight important words, phrases, or sentences.
- Create special symbols to place beside information to indicate your level of understanding and ability to use the ideas. The symbols give personal feedback and guide self-talk. Examples could include:

  **   I understand this information.

  ^ ^   I need more explanation here.

  ??   I have a question.

  !!   I will use this information.

Tips for Creating Research Note Cards

Note cards are used to take notes from a source as the learner gathers research information. The sources are identified on a card because the information must be cited accurately if it is used later in the text or bibliography. Guidelines for completing research note cards include

- Record information needed for the report.
- Use the back of the card or another card, if needed.
- Begin each new source with a new card.
- Use your own words to record the information.
- Keep cards from the same source together.

Sample Note Card

Name _____ Teacher _____ Date _____

Topic _____

Source _____ Date of Publication _____

Title _____ Page Number _____

Information gathered:

TEACHER'S ROLE IN NOTE TAKING

- Model each strategy.
- Share examples.
- Explain purposes and uses of this information-gathering technique.
- Differentiate the various forms of note taking for the different research resources used, which may include encyclopedias, magazines, reference texts, and the Internet.

DEVELOPING OUTLINES AND RUBRICS

On Line With Outlines

Begin the student with his first outline experiences using lines for the subheadings. The process of filling in the blanks during oral lessons or study sessions provides the learner with successful experiences in his introduction to outlining.

EXAMPLE

Parts of a Flower

I. Roots   II. Stem
A. _____   A. _____
        1. _____   1. _____
        2. _____   2. _____
        3. _____

B. _____   B. _____
        1. _____   1. _____
        2. _____   2. _____

Rubrics

Use the following rubric to indicate the amount of information you have on each subtopic. Use this form to monitor the writer's research progress. Ask the student to place an X on the line to indicate the amount of information he has found on each subtopic.

Subtopic   **Teeny Tiny ---------- Gracious Plenty ----------**

1. _____   ←--→
2. _____   ←--→
3. _____   ←--→

So far, I have used the following sources: _____ _____ _____
I plan to use _____.
I am looking for _____.

Research Rubric

The following rubric may be used for a self-evaluation on a research assignment.

Ask the student to place an X on the line to indicate his self-evaluation of each item.

	In the Trenches	**Over the Rainbow**
1. Collected data	←--→	
2. Used sources effectively	←--→	
3. Created note cards fitting the criteria	←--→	
4. Recorded data accurately	←--→	
5. Met the timeline for the project	←--→	

Comments:

WRITING ESSAYS

This graphic organizer categorizes and records gathered information in an organized way. After plotting the data, the student writes his paper using these categories to begin the drafting. Many essays follow this five-point approach to writing paragraphs (see Figure 5.3).

Organizing a Five-Paragraph Essay

Try one of the graphics shown in Figures 5.4, 5.5, 5.6, and 5.7 to organize an essay. Note the different shape used for each part. Use a variety of shapes to make the ideas easier to follow. Link the shape to the information recorded on it. Discuss each shape and its role. Remember, the categories are examples. They may be changed and adapted to the content information.

Handy Dandy Essays

Plan your five paragraphs in this Handy Dandy way!
A. Place the topic in the palm of the hand or a glove.
B. Place the main idea on the thumb. That is the Whoop-Di-Do first paragraph.
C. Repeat that main idea in different words on the little finger. It is important to repeat the main idea or topic in the conclusion. This is the last paragraph.
D. Write a supporting detail on each middle finger. These are the three middle paragraphs.

Figure 5.3　A Five-Point Approach to Writing Paragraphs

Beginning
Name the topic or subject.
Make opening comments.
Use a hook to get the audience's attention.
Introduce the characters, scene, and plot.
Use the surprise element.
Create curiosity. Ask a question.
Bring in the readers' emotions.
Set the stage. Describe the scene.
Introduce the characters.
Write as though you are speaking directly to the reader.
Use a quote.
Use an anecdote or example.
Use unique or interesting information or trivia (facts).
Make an unbelievable or "far out" statement.

Middle
Give main points and details.
Use subtopic paragraphs.
Support the subject.
Stay on your topic.
Build the plot or purpose.
Place details in order.
Group details together.

Ending
Make conclusions: Tie up loose ends.
Review or summarize the most important ideas.
Express your overall feelings, thoughts, or conclusions.
Restate the topic in the beginning paragraph.
Tell how the plot was resolved.
Provide a solution.
Make a recommendation.
Repeat the main points in a new way.
Take the reader back to the beginning.

BEGINNING

SUBTOPIC A

SUBTOPIC B

SUBTOPIC C

ENDING

Figure 5.4　From Beginning to End

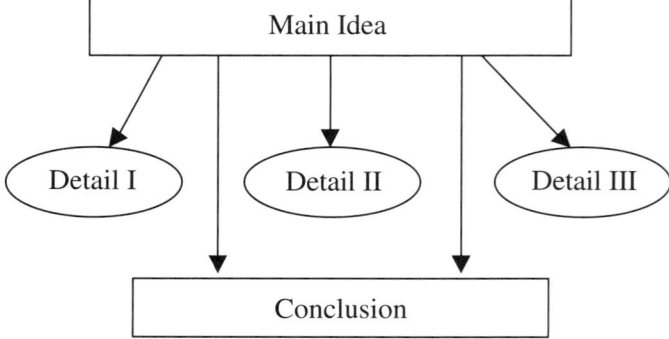

Main Idea

Detail I　　Detail II　　Detail III

Conclusion

Figure 5.5 The Five W's

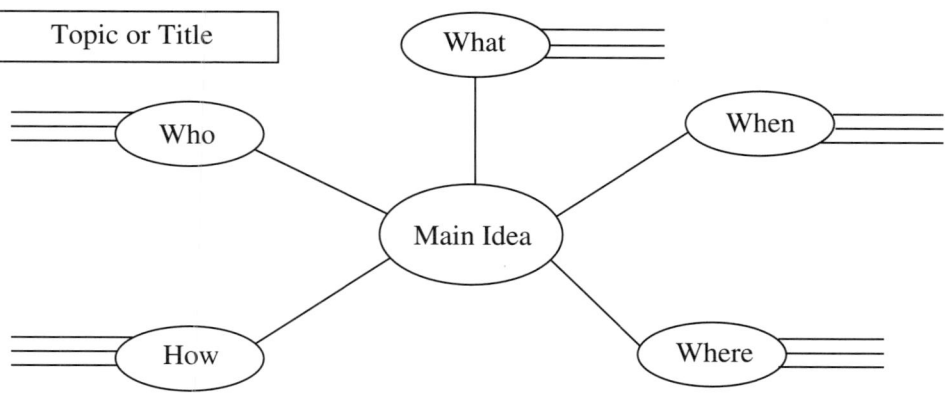

Figure 5.6 Shape Talk

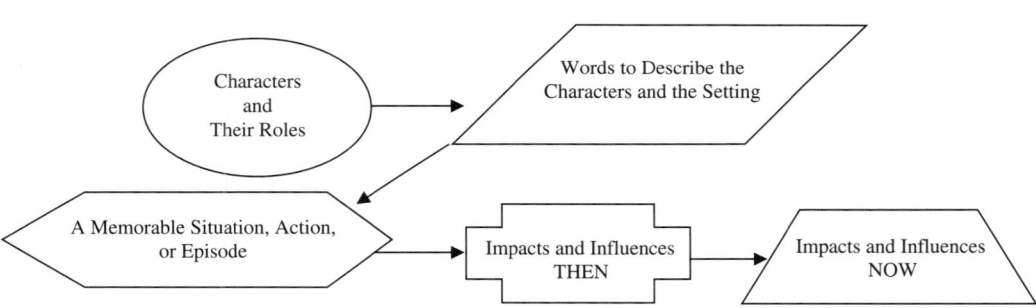

Figure 5.7 Persuasive Writing

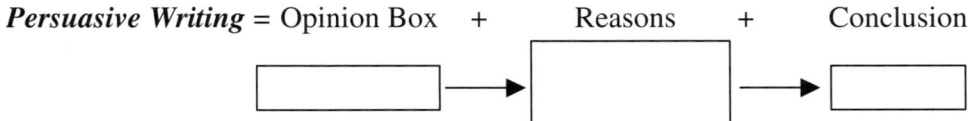

Stretch Your Main Ideas

Essay Checklist

Use this checklist as a self-analysis. It is an effective tool to use during or after a revision or editing session.

Author _____   Date _____

Organization
____ My information is told in order.
____ Each paragraph has a main idea and supporting details.

Sentence Structure
____ A variety of sentences is used.
____ Each sentence has a complete thought.
____ I use the best words to express my meaning.

Details/Main Idea
____ All details tell about the subject.
____ I have enough details to give needed information.

Style
____ My story is easy to read.
____ The writing form is consistent.
____ Many words will activate the readers' senses.
____ Words are used to stir emotions.
____ Dialogue is used.
____ Adjectives and adverbs create vivid mental pictures.

Mechanics
____ All sentences begin with a capital letter.
____ The correct punctuation is used.
____ Spelling errors are corrected.

Comments

RHYMES AND RIDDLES

Students enjoy using content information to create rhymes and riddles. Relevant data, facts, and concepts are easily remembered when they are processed in these creative ways. Adapt the following examples for the student to use with content information.

Limerick

Five lines
Lines 1, 2, and 5 must
rhyme.
Lines 3 and 4 must rhyme.

Example
My thoughts are written in black
and white.
On paper my ideas are quite a sight!
No one has thoughts just like mine.
Words spill out of my head line by line.
I am an author each time I write.

A–D Time

Lines 1–4 must begin
with A–D.
Line 5 may begin with
any letter.

Example
Alligators glide through the sand.
Birds dance on the water's edge.
Crabs crawl over broken shells.
Dragonflies flock at dusk.
Nature's creatures take careless risks.

Ballad

A ballad tells a story.
It is written in four-line
stanzas.
Lines 2 and 4 rhyme.

Example
Did you know Davy Crockett?
He fought with Texas against Mexico.
He was a Tennessee volunteer.
He died at the Alamo.

Couplet

A couplet has two lines
that rhyme.

Example
President Carter received the
Nobel Peace Prize
For promoting world peace in our lives.

One-to-One Dynamite

Line
1 One noun
2 Two adjectives to describe
3 Three action verbs
4 Two adjectives
5 Three action verbs
6 Two adjectives to describe
the noun on line 7
7 One noun

Example
Peace
Democratic, tranquil
Surrounds, calms, spreads
Chaotic, bloody
Invades, scares, destroys
Chemical, biological

War

Riddles

Riddles give hints to a specific answer. The statements are written as clues to solve a thought - provoking question or statement.

Sample Riddle 1

I wore small glasses.

I was a patriot in the American Revolution.

I discovered electricity while flying a kite.

Who am I? _____

Answer: Benjamin Franklin

Sample Riddle 2

I am a famous dance.

I am created with spins and other graceful movements.

The *Nutcracker,* a fantasy-filled Christmas story, is told with my moves.

Dancers must be on their toes to display my art form.

What am I? _____

Answer: Ballet

POETRY ADAPTATIONS FOR CONTENT

Well-known poems provide patterns for creative use of content information. Lines from famous poetry may be used as models to apply knowledge gained from the topic.

Examples

"Stopping by Woods on a Snowy Evening" by Robert Frost
Whose woods these are
  I think I know.
His house is in the village though.

Adaptation for Problem Solving
The answer here
I soon will know.
I just follow the steps as I go.

"Trees" by Joyce Kilmer
I think that I shall never see
A poem as lovely as a tree.

Adaptation for History
I think that I shall never see
A general as famous as
  Robert E. Lee.

"Fog" by Carl Sandburg
The fog comes on little cat feet.
It sits looking
Over harbor and city
On silent haunches
And then moves on.

Adaptation for Science:
   "Icy Rain"
The sleet glides on big bear paws.
It starts pouring
Over glaciers and mountains
On stinging free falls
Then slinks away.

GETTING TO KNOW TEXT CHARACTERS

When children write stories, they imagine characters and construct themselves as human beings at the same time.

—(Graves, 1999)

Use the following activities in all curriculum areas to explore famous people of yesterday or today. The character strategies are designed to showcase the students' knowledge. The students' level of success reflects their ability to adapt the information

Content Character Connections

1. Identify the characters studied.
   Ask students to number off to match the number of characters. For example, if five characters are identified, the students number off with 1, 2, 3, 4, 5/1, 2, 3, 4, 5. Continue to number off until all students have a number.

2. The learners who have number 1 form a group and work together. The learners who have number 2 form a group and work together. Continue until all groups are formed.

3. Assign a character to each group.

4. Individual group members gather the information for the assigned character.

5. The group compiles the individual data, decides what information will be reported and how to present it.

6. Each group member has a role in the presentation.

7. The group gathers props and artifacts.

8. Rehearse the performances and present.

Encourage the audience to take notes, ask questions, and discuss each character with the information learned.

Character Research

The following guide is used with students as they begin research experiences with important people in the topic of study.

1. Name of character

2. Adjective, adjective, adjective

3. I liked _____ because _____.

or

I did not like _____ because _____.

4. I will remember this person because _____

_____.

Character Trace

1. Draw a large outline of the character studied.

2. Label and dress the character to illustrate the character's interests and personality. Include items to reflect the time period.

3. Display the character. Learn and enjoy!

Note: Teachers who have several classes may choose one character for a total class project. Competition may be created between the classes to make the assignment more challenging. These characters make excellent hall and door decorations.

Character Comparisons

_____ and _____ are two important people in _____.
_____ is _____, while _____ is _____. I think both characters _____.

Famous Person Showcase

1. Make a life-sized replica of the famous person or character studied.

2. Create outfits for the character from available items, scrap material, or clothes from home.

3. Stuff the clothing with newspaper or rags.

4. Go on a Scavenger Hunt to find facts and trivia related to the assigned character.

5. Surround the character with artifacts, music, and other information to portray his traits, experiences, and contributions.

6. Plan the most effective way to present the information.

7. Present the report in a unique way to reflect the person's importance and personality.

8. Celebrate!

Characters in the Content Scene

This activity teaches students how to mentally process information through creative writing. Use the grid in Figure 5.8 to create characters that interact with the content information.

1. Choose a genre for the activity. Select a character from the Character column.

2. Use a spinner or roll the dice to select the character's attribute, the time, his feelings, the place, and a companion.

3. Situate the character in the selected genre to interact with information learned in the unit of study. Emphasize the importance of using correct facts and details.

Figure 5.8 Create a Character

	Character	Attributes	Time	Feelings	Place	Companion
1	Old man	tall	long ago	scared	beach	friend
2	Young lady	short	now	angry	mall	dog
3	Toddler	adventurous	later	sad	park	teenager
4	Baby	happy	tomorrow	afraid	woods	lion
5	Young boy	sad	yesterday	sleepy	cave	partner
6	Teenager	sneaky	earlier	happy	tent	sister

EXAMPLE

> **Character created:** young lady tall yesterday angry park friend
>
> **Content:** equivalent fractions
>
> **Placing the character in the content scene:**

Yesterday I saw a tall young lady walking in the park with a friend. They stopped to rest and share a nutritious snack bar. As they broke it in half, an angry teenaged girl ran up to them to ask for directions to the exit.

She was lost. They offered her a portion of their snack bar. Each friend broke her half of the bar into thirds, making a total of 6 pieces and gave the jogger 2 pieces. Each person had 2/6 or 1/3 of the snack.

Character Spotlight

A screen script is a story written for a movie. It may be based on a true story or come from your imagination. Choose an interesting character and plot. Divide the story into three acts.

Act I

1. Introduce the characters.

2. Describe the heroine or main character, so the audience will want to cheer for her.

3. Grab the readers' attention with an exciting action or event.

4. Create a problem or a struggle for the main character.

Act II

1. Present the character's attempts to overcome the struggle or problem.

2. Describe the character's move toward being a heroine or solving her problems.

3. Present another conflict or problem as this act ends.

Act III

1. Explain the character's actions as the problem is solved.

2. Describe the heroine's return to a normal or happy life.

Figure 5.9   Reflection on a Stick

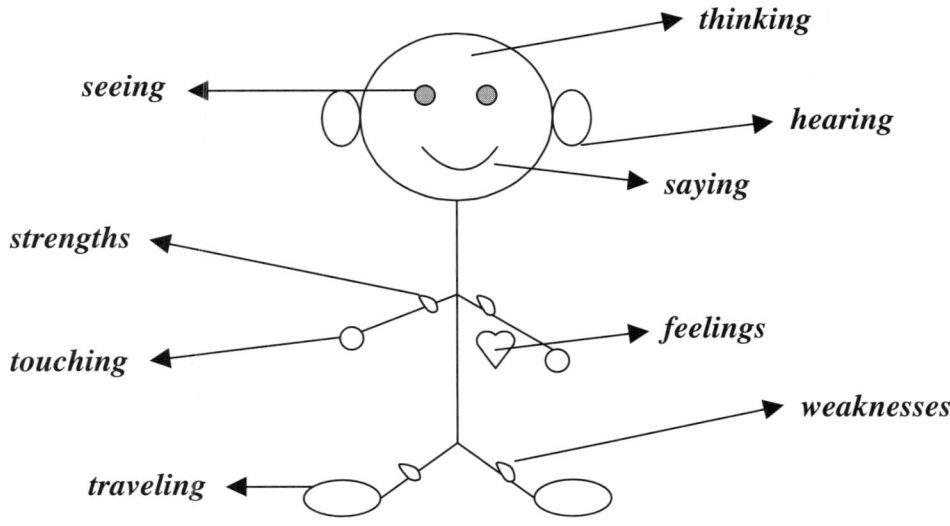

Reflections on a Stick

1. Ask each group to draw a stick figure on a piece of paper.

2. Place three or four of the following terms around the stick figure for students to brainstorm in relation to the important person or character: seeing, thinking, hearing, saying, strengths, touching, feelings, traveling and weaknesses. See Figure 5.9 for an example of a guides for reflections on a stick.

More Character Activities

- Create a song, riddle, jingle, rap, or cheer about a character's life.
- Log the events in the character's life.
- Describe what it would have been like to live during the time of this person.
- Make a speech as the character.
- Create a choral reading to tell about the character's life.
- Write about the character as a newspaper reporter or a critic.
- Develop a job description for the character.

WRITING FROM A TO Z

Students respond to new and unique activities. In *How the Brain Learns* (2001), David Sousa states that the brain has a "persistent interest in novelty" (p. 27), that is, to changes occurring in the environment. Unique experiences improve the brain's ability to store and to search for information. Teachers should use a variety of teaching and writing strategies in novel ways to stay out of teaching ruts! Novelty is an effective motivational tool to use with content information because it generates excitement and enjoyment in the learning process. This is an effective motivational tool to use with character builders or self-improvement activities because it will focus attention and develop a learner who eagerly looks forward to writing activities.

The following focus activities may be used with content information across the curriculum. They are designed to use before, during, or after content lessons. The activities provide novel ways for the teacher to check for understanding as the students apply information learned. These differentiated experiences also can provide opportunities for learners to enjoy writing and to grow as authors.

Alliteration

1. Choose a letter of the alphabet.

2. Brainstorm words with the same beginning sound.

3. Write alliterations related to the content information with the words that begins with the same sound.

Example: People pollute ponds pitching paper plates.

Brain Bash

1. Work in teams of three or four students.

2. List all possible responses to a question related to the topic of study.

3. Set a 2–3 minute time limit for brainstorming.

4. Choose one group member as the recorder to write the brainstormed list.

5. Praise the group with the longest accurate list.

6. Compile the responses on a chart or overhead.

EXAMPLES

How many objects can you name that are shaped like a rectangle?

What can be poured from a bottle?

How many flying animals can you name?

Crack the Code

Write important facts in a special code. The simplest code uses letters of the alphabet in sequence. Students enjoy creating challenging codes.

1 2 3 4 5 6 7 8 9 10 11 12 13 14 15 16 17 18 19 20 21 22 23 24 25 26
A B C D E F G H I J K L M N O P Q R S T U V W X Y Z

Decipher this message using the code above (Asterisks separate words.)

23-18-9-20-9-14-7*19-20 18-1-20-5-7-9-5-19*3-1-14*2-5*21-19-5-4*9-14*1-12-12*3-15-14-20-5-14-20*1-18-5-1-19.

Answer: _____

Community Connections

Plan writing activities related to the unit of study to involve the community. Students make personal connections with individuals, agencies, and groups in the local area through their writing experiences. Try these communication ideas:

- Write notes to veterans, politicians, or important leaders.
- Create placemats with special notes and poems for nursing homes.
- Invite a government official to share the role of writing in his job.
- Write a biography for an important individual or role model. Plan a celebration to honor this person.
- Conduct investigations and write possible solutions to environmental concerns.
- Write about the cultures of the people in the community to honor the diversity.

Dear Author

Write to the textbook author. This experience will focus students' attention on the value of the information in the text and develop letter-writing skills. Guide writers with the following statements and questions:

1. I like this textbook because_____.

2. You could improve this text by _____.

3. Why did you write about _____ in this chapter?

4. Why didn't you include _____?

5. I learned from you that _____.

6. It would help students if you _____ in your next book.

7. The part I liked best in the book was _____.

Dreaming

Choose a topic, object, concept, or vocabulary word from the unit of study and write a metaphor about dreaming.

Example: If I were the _____, I would _____.
If I were the <u>diameter</u>, I would <u>feel strong because I could cross the center of a circle at any point and know that my line would cut the circle in half.</u>

Egg on Your Face

"Egg on your face" is an expression used to describe a feeling of deep embarrassment.

1. Think of a time when you had "egg on your face."

2. Describe the events that led to the embarrassment.

3. Explain exactly how you felt.

4. What advice would you give someone who has egg on his face?

Eyewitness Accounts

An eyewitness account is a report prepared by a person "on the scene." He reveals everything he viewed, heard, and felt. This activity provides practice with sequencing, organization of thoughts, and details to describe events or happenings.

Use this expository writing activity within units of study to show young authors how to make events, characters, and scenes vivid in the readers' minds. Tell the authors to record the information as a reporter for a live newscast.

EXAMPLES

Topic	Reporter
Pollination	Bee
A historical battle	Soldier
Oceanography	Shark

Measurement   Yardstick
Sports   Volleyball
Computer technology   Mouse

Fact Frames

Fact Frames organize information in the unit of study using illustrations.

1. List the facts.

2. Identify the number of frames needed to illustrate the facts.

3. Draw one illustration for each Fact Frame.

4. Write or list the important facts around each picture in graffiti style.

5. Organize the Fact Frames in sequential order.

Fit as a Fiddle

The phrase "fit as a fiddle" means "in good health."

1. What would someone do to stay "fit as a fiddle"?

2. Describe what you would hear if someone played a fiddle that was "not fit."

3. Write a "fit as a fiddle" rap.

Flip It

Make a Flip Book to record information. Use three sheets of paper. Follow these directions:

1. Crease and fold down one-fourth of the first sheet of paper.

2. Crease and fold down one-half of the second sheet of paper.

3. Crease and fold down three-fourths of the third sheet of paper.

4. Slide the folded end of the paper with one-half folded inside the fold on the paper with the one-fourth crease.

5. Slide the paper with the three-fourths crease folded inside the one-half fold.

6. Staple the papers together on the fold.

7. Write the title for the Flip Book on the top fold.

8. Write related information on other pages created in the Flip Book.

Get It to Go!

Challenge students to write questions from the unit of study with one-word answers. Tell students to write each question on a separate card with the answer on the back of the card. Use the cards in the following activity:

This game is effective with small groups or the total class. Arrange seats in a circle so the Challenger moves quickly and easily behind each participant's chair. Choose the first Challenger. The Challenger stands behind the first seated student to challenge him to "Get It" first. Use these directions to guide the game.

1. Ask a question from the cards written by students.

2. The seated student and the Challenger compete to answer the question or be the one to "Get It" or say the correct answer first. The seated student must say the correct answer before the Challenger says it.

    *   If the seated student says the answer correctly before the Challenger or student standing, he takes the Challenger's place. The Challenger sits in the vacated chair.

    *   If the seated student and the Challenger say the correct answer at the same time the Challenger maintains his "To Go" position and moves behind the next student's chair.

    *   Each member of the class or group listens to questions and responses until the Challenger is standing behind his chair.

3. The "Get It" Challenger continues to move behind each student and challenge him to challenge the student in front of him. The Challenger takes the winner's chair. The winning student becomes the Challenger and stands behind the next student ready for the next question.

4. The object of the game is for the Challenger to "Get It" or answer each question before the student seated in front of him answers it.

5. If the Challenger or standing student says the answer correctly first or can "Get It", he moves behind the chair of the next student to challenge him.

6. The Challenger earns a point each time he can answer a question or "Gets It To Go".

    Note: Simple word problems and all content area facts may be written by students for a "Get It To Go" game.

Hitch Your Wagon to a Star

The phrase, "Hitch your wagon to a star," advises someone to aim high and follow his dreams.

1. List your talents or strengths.

2. How can you use your talents or strengths to "hitch" your dreams to a star?

3. What can you do to improve and use your talents and strengths?

If I Were in His Shoes

Put yourself in the place of a character and try some of the following sentence starters:

- If I were as famous as _____, I would _____.
- If I were _____ and I could become invisible, I would _____.
- If I could spend the day with _____, I would _____.

In the Spotlight

Choose a person in the passage or unit of study to recognize or honor. Answer the following questions. Design a certificate, medal, badge, or plaque to honor the person in the spotlight.

1. The star in my story is _____. Why? _____

2. I want to honor _____ because _____.

3. I can describe this person as being _____, _____, _____, and _____.

4. If I could award _____ with a special title, it would be _____.

Jump on the Bandwagon

"Jump on the bandwagon" is a phrase used to ask someone to join an activity because other people are in it. The earliest bandwagons were pulled by horses. Bands played on the wagons to encourage people to join them in support of a particular person.

Answer the following questions:

1. When is it a good idea to "jump on the bandwagon"?

2. When would it be dangerous to "jump on the bandwagon"?

3. What are some things friends might say to convince you to join them on the bandwagon?

4. Describe a time when you decided that you should not "jump on a bandwagon."

Keepsakes

A keepsake is a special item you treasure and want to keep.

1. Create a list of your keepsakes.

2. What makes each keepsake a special treasure?

3. How did you receive your favorite keepsake?

Last Blast

Choose one of the following prompts. Write all about it.

The last movie I saw _____.

The last time I ate in a restaurant _____.

The last time I visited with a friend, we _____.

The last time I went shopping, I came home with _____.

The last time I had fun with a friend was when _____.

The last time I received a prized possession, I was _____.

The last time I felt excited was when _____.

The last thing that made me giggle was _____.

Look Who's Talking

1. Write an imaginary conversation taking place between you and a character or an important person in the unit of study.

EXAMPLE

Student: "Hello, Columbus! How did you feel when you met the Indians?"

Columbus: "Well, Billy, it was strange and exciting. I called the people Indians, because I thought I had reached India."

2. Choose two concepts from the unit of study. Assign each concept to a student. Tell each student to take on the role of the concept and talk to each other.

EXAMPLE

Latitude and Longitude are having a conversation:

Longitude exclaims: "Hey Latitude! Look at me! All of my lines cross the equator, the hottest place on Earth."

Latitude responds: "Well, you don't have very much to brag about. My zero line is on the hot equator at all times. How tough do you think that line has to be?"

3. Ask students to write a conversation with two animals, insects, objects, or people in the unit of study.

EXAMPLES

Pluto and Jupiter	A root and a stem	Popcorn and soda
Lightning and thunder	A square and an octagon	A ball and a bat
A diameter and a radius	A nickel and a dollar	A disk and a computer

Mailbox

Designate a special container for student and teacher correspondence. Display directions and topic suggestions for writing the communications. Use the box for suggestions, questions, or notes to the teacher. She reads and answers the mail.

Musical Facts

Create a song that includes three to five facts in the study. Use a familiar tune, so the students do not struggle with the tune. Emphasis should be on the information.

EXAMPLE

Fact or Opinion
(Tune: "Mary Had a Little Lamb")
A fact is the truth with evidence you know,
Evidence you know, evidence you know
A fact is the truth with evidence you know.
So always search for the facts.

An opinion is a belief you can take or let go.
Take or let go, take or let go
An opinion is a belief you can take or let go
So choose your opinions wisely.

My Swaying Ways

Persuasion sways or changes beliefs. The following guidelines are used to teach persuasive writing skills:

1. Choose a topic or issue that directly affects students.

   EXAMPLES

Computer time	In-class movies
Snack machines in the cafeteria	Wearing uniforms in school
Hall passes	Longer school days
Selecting a new mascot design	More free play or breaks

2. Write your personal opinion on the topic.

3. Survey others to find out how they feel about the topic. Gather their opinions to show that there is more than one side to the issue. Ask them to state their beliefs or point of view on the topic or issue.

4. Write your platform or beliefs. Explain why you have these beliefs.

5. Draw a conclusion stating your feelings or opinions.

6. Use your feelings and opinions to sway others to your side of the issue.

Note Play

Take notes on newscasts, movies, favorite television shows, and documentaries to provide practice with note taking. Get together with peers and discuss the most useful notes.

Choose one of the following areas to rewrite:

The dialogue   A character's role   The plot   The setting   The ending

Pictogram

Choose a shape from the unit of study. Create an outline for the shape using words, phrases, sentences, paragraphs, or poetry related to the topic.

Quiz Whiz

Write trivia questions related to the topic of study on individual index cards. Write the answers on the back of each card. Use the cards to create a game.

Smart Shirt

Design a T-shirt to detail a vocabulary word, a topic, an event, region, a setting, or a person being studied.

EXAMPLE

1. Write the name of the geographic region in the center of the shirt.
2. Write an adjective to describe the region directly below the name of the region.
3. Write the natural resources in the bottom right corner.
4. Write interesting trivia in the bottom left corner.
5. Record the physical features on one sleeve.
6. List major cities on the other sleeve.

The Eyes Have It

Choose a place or thing. Personify it by giving a related object nearby the eyes to describe the place or thing.

SUGGESTIONS

A grain of sand describing the beach

A wheel spoke describing a bicycle

A net describing a basketball game

A saddle describing a horse

A book describing an author.

This Is My Life

Timelines place events in sequential order using a scale of dates. They may be used to view the life of an individual or events in the unit of study.

The following activity may be used to introduce timelines. Students enjoy sharing important events in their lives. Use a strip of paper or adding machine tape. Ask students to create timelines for highlights in their life.

EXAMPLE

0	5	7	14	17
Birth	Disneyland	Swimming Lesson	Soccer Trophy	Driver's License

Through My Eyes

Write a story in First Person to share a personal experience you have had:

In a car	In your yard	On a trip
While eating	During the night	On an adventure

Figure 5.10 Triangle Tricks. Answer: Row 6=DETAIL; Row 5=ELATE; Row 4=TALE; Row 3=ATE; Row 2=AT; Row 1=A

1.

2.

3.

4.

5.

6.

Triangle Tricks

Use Figure 5.10 in this activity.

1. Begin by selecting a word to fit in the boxes on the bottom row.
2. Drop one letter of the original word. Rearrange the letters to create a new word in the boxes above the original word.
3. Continue this procedure until you reach the box at the top of the triangle.
4. Try this trick and then make up your own.

Up a Creek Without a Paddle

Ask students if they have ever been in so much trouble that they believed there was no way out of it. If they have had this experience, they have been "up a creek without a paddle."

1. What kind of trouble did you get into that left you "up a creek without a paddle"?
2. What did you try to do to get yourself out of trouble?
3. What did you learn from the event?

Upset the Applecart

Ask students if anyone has ever had something or someone to interfere with their exciting activities or plans.

1. Describe an exciting plan or event that had to end because someone or something "upset your applecart."
2. How did you react to the accident or surprise that made your plans or activities change?

Vamoose

Vamoose is a slang term that means "to leave a place quickly."

1. List places that gave you the feeling that you needed to vamoose or leave as soon as possible.
2. Why were you there?
3. Did you have to stay and deal with the vamoose feelings?
4. Explain how you feel when you have to be somewhere you don't want to be.

VIP

Pronounce each letter in *VIP*. This is an acronym for "Very Important Person."

1. Describe a VIP you know.

2. What makes this person a VIP?

3. How are you a VIP for a friend, a pet, or a family member?

Vocabulary Predictions

Use the following writing activity to reinforce vocabulary words as they are introduced, to make predictions related to new information, and to create examples of the writing and reading connection (Fisher, 1998; McGinley & Denner, 1987). The teacher can list five to seven key vocabulary words, names, and phrases from the story, or content information. Challenge students to use the key words and terms in a paragraph in the next unit of study.

EXAMPLE

Vocabulary words: kangaroo   Australia   Ayers Rock   Great Barrier Reef

Prediction: We are going to study the continent of Australia. As we study we will learn about the sea creatures in the Great Barrier Reef. We will learn why Ayers Rock is important. We will learn about the kangaroos. I hope we learn how long a baby kangaroo stays in his mother's pouch.

Walk on Eggshells

This phrase means "to be very careful."

1. Think of a time when you had to "walk on eggshells" or be very careful about what you said to someone.

2. Describe the occasion.

3. When is it important to "walk on eggshells" while talking to someone?

Writing Olympics

Tell students they are going to have a race to see who can write the most words within the time limit as they participate in free writing.

1. Choose a topic for the Writing Olympics. Set a timer.

2. Write about your topic during the 2–3-minute time limit.

3. Count the number of words you wrote.

4. Celebrate with the winners and share the writing.

Note: Increase the time limit with each Writing Olympic activity.

X Out

This phrase means to mark out or delete by placing the letter *X* over a word, phrase, sentence, or object.

1. Write about an object or activity you would like to "X Out" of your life.

2. Why is this object or activity part of your life now?

3. Why do you want to "X Out" this object or activity?

Yum Yum

1. List foods you like to eat.

2. Choose your favorite food from the list.

3. Write everything you know about your favorite food.

4. Describe how and when you like to eat your favorite food.

Zone In Reflections

1. The students list the pluses of today's lesson on a sticky note.

2. The students list the minuses of the lesson, if there are any, on a separate sticky note. Use different colored markers or sticky notes for the pluses and the minuses.

3. The teacher places a plus sign or the words "Pluses of the Lesson" on the left side of the door facing.

4. Place a minus sign or the words "Minuses of the Lesson" on the right side of the door facing.

5. Ask students to place their notes on the proper door facing as they leave the learning zone.

The "Zone In Reflection" is the ticket from the room.

Curriculum Approaches for the Differentiated Writing Classroom

6

A butterfly charts his individual course.
The young author chooses his writing destiny.

Teachers make a difference in the writing journey of each life they touch. Content teachers in the differentiated writing classroom who plan their students' writing experiences with careful attention to each student's individual needs. They develop and support effective young authors whose skills will last a lifetime.

CHOICE BOARDS

Use Choice Boards for students to select various ways to work with their information. The following are samples of Choice Boards. The Wild Card space is used for students who want to think of other ways that they might prefer to work with the information. When a student chooses a Wild Card, his idea is approved by the teacher. The approval request may be placed in a Choice submission basket on the teacher's desk.

EXAMPLE

1. Name_____ Date _____ Topic _____

2. Student: My Wild Card activity pick is _____ .

3. Teacher approval: _____ Yes ___ No *(Check one)*

4. Teacher Signature or Initials: _____ Dates: _____

Writing Thinking Boxes

This Choice Board shown in Figure 6.1 is designed to reach different levels of thinking to differentiate assignments. These offerings challenge students to use their high-level thinking skills while developing problem solvers and thinkers.

Figure 6.1   Writing Thinking Boxes

Level I: Knowledge	**Level II: Comprehension**
• Write the step-by-step sequence of a procedure or event. • Tell about it in your own words.	• Interpret and illustrate the story in your own words. • Name some examples.
Level III: Application	**Level IV: Analysis**
• Demonstrate a way to use _____. • Organize the data.	• If _____, then ____. • Make a graph using the information.
Level V: Synthesis	**Level VI: Evaluation**
• Write an original plan. • Develop a new way.	• Design an ad for the best use of a product. • Create an evaluation and decide how it will benefit others.

Bingo Choice

The sample Choice Board shown in Figure 6.2 gives students options of different ways to write. Selections are chosen from the board. The board is designed like the game BINGO. The student or the teacher selects activities to complete.

Choice Tic Tac Toe

Figure 6.3 is another example of a Choice Board for an Agenda assignment or writing time at a center. The student selects one activity on the board to complete over a period of time or chooses a row to complete.

"It" Board

The sample Choice Board shown in Figure 6.4 is on a specific topic, concept, or vocabulary word. These generic selections can be used across the content areas.

AGENDAS

Agendas are given to students who need individual, specific assignments. The Agenda is designed for the student who does not need to work on the total group's activities. Assignments teach the standards on the student's ability level using stimulating, challenging activities in his area of interest. Busy work is not included. A timeline is set for completion of the work. As each task is completed, it may be placed in an Agenda folder. The student keeps a checklist or reflection log in the folder. The reflections may be useful as assessment pieces. An Agenda may be part of an approved contract that addresses the learner's diverse needs. Examples of ideas for Agendas are continued on page 143.

Figure 6.2 BINGO Choice Board]

	A	B	C	D	E
1	Create a cartoon showing conversation between a movie hero and a fairy-tale character.	Choose a television show you would recommend to everyone. Write a review of the show. Tell why you selected the show.	Write an advertising jingle about your favorite food.	Think of a new invention to help you study. Draw it. Write a description for a magazine article.	Write the directions to your favorite sport or hobby. Illustrate it.
2	List five of your favorite books. Rewrite the ending for one of the books.	Pretend you are interviewing your hero on a talk show. Write a script for the show.	Create a Flip Book to describe the many uses for an empty can. Illustrate each page.	Use a Venn Diagram to compare and contrast two of your favorite pastimes.	Create a poster to "sell" your friends on reading a favorite book.
3	You are a millionaire for a day. Write a one-day entry for a diary that tells about your lucky day.	Design a postcard that describes your town. Write a note on the card telling someone why he should visit you.	WILD CARD	If you were twice as tall, what would you do? Write a poem about your adventures.	Find your favorite topic in the encyclopedia. Make an outline for the topic.

Figure 6.2 (Continued)

	A	B	C	D	E
4	Survey your classmates about their favorite ice cream flavors. Create a chart with the results. Write a summary for the class newsletter.	Write a newspaper article about your greatest fear.	Name a wild animal found in your state. Create a concept map related to the animal.	If you could change one part of your day, what would it be? Explain your reasons.	Read about your favorite pet. Create a Shape Book to tell about the pet.
5	Develop your platform to persuade your parents to buy you the new game you want.	Invent a new way to do the chore that you dislike the most.	Write a training manual to teach someone the way to play your favorite sport or game.	Create a PowerPoint presentation about your school, home, town, or state.	Write a song to a familiar tune, rap, or poem that describes facts about a person, place or thing we are studying.

Figure 6.3 Choice Tic Tac Toe

	A	B	C
1	Design a bookmark with a list of your favorite book characters.	List three things you like about a room in our house. Write a note to your mom telling her how you would like to change the room.	Name your favorite vehicle. Use ten words to describe how it moves.
2	Write a note telling someone why he or she is special.	WILD CARD	Write a poem about your favorite television program.
3	Read about your favorite animal. Draw it. Write five sentences that tell why it would or would not be a good pet.	Name an insect you see often. See how much you can learn about the insect. Draw it. Label the insect's parts.	Choose three objects in your classroom. Write three short sentences as "What Am I?" clues for the objects. Ask a friend to guess your objects from the clues.

Figure 6.4 "It" Board

	A	B	C
1	Draw and label it.	Write a poem about it.	Compare it with something else.
2	Write to someone and persuade them that they need it.	WILD CARD	Name it and write an ad to sell it.
3	Write a story or play making it the main character.	Pretend it just became a new member of our class. Write a set of rules that it must follow.	Create a best friend for it. Write a conversation between the two at their first meeting.

Examples of agenda ideas:

- Complete a computer program.
- Listen to a taped piece of information. Then write a summary, critique, or editorial for the piece.
- Plot information on a graphic organizer. Then write or draw the sequence of events or procedures for an experiment using the organizer.
- Complete a list of three to five writing activities within a specific period of time.
- Generate a list of activities for the individual or small group to complete.
- Select a row or column of writing activities from a Choice Board.

There are many advantages for using an Agenda with a student. The writing assignments are designed to match the student's individual needs. He is able to work at his own pace. The learner chooses the task order. He has a set period of time to complete the tasks. The independent work fosters self-directed learning.

INDIVIDUALIZED WRITING PROJECTS

An alternative assignment sometimes becomes an independent writing project. A project has a set goal and purpose. Sometimes the project is assigned with an essential question to answer, hypothesis to prove, or problem to solve. The project gives the learner an opportunity to gain in-depth knowledge of a topic. The topic or subtopic is selected by the student with a contract, from a Choice Board, or the teacher assigns it. An established timeline and rubric are set at the beginning of the project, so that expectations are determined. To accompany the written requirement, the student needs the opportunity to demonstrate the learning and under-standing gained from the project with a performance assessment. Examples of such an assessment include a graphic, a musical composition, a role-play, or an interview. For additional information on contracts, brainstorming, researching, and note taking, see these sections in Chapter 5.

Project Rubric

Student _____ Date _____

Project Assignment _____

Rater: ____ Self ____ Peer ____ Teacher

Accuracy of Information

<--->
2   4   6   8

Research Gathered

<--->
2   4   6   8

Timeline Followed

<--->
2   4   6   8

Presentation Debut

<--->
2   4   6   8

Overall Project

<--->
2   4   6   8

Comments About the Project

Rater	Student

Rater's Signature _____   Date _____

Student's Signature _____   Date _____

LESSON PLANNING MODEL FOR WRITING IN THE CONTENT AREAS

Many decisions are made as lessons are designed with writing activities. Lesson planning must cover strategies and ideas to meet students' needs (A) before, (B) during, and (C) after their writing experiences.

The following are questions to consider when developing an effective writing lesson.

A. *Before Writing*

The Topic

1. What is this group's background knowledge on this topic?

2. Which pre-assessment tools will I use?

3. How will I "hook" students into wanting to write?

Purpose of the Assignment

1. What is the purpose of this writing assignment?

2. Which standards, concepts, objectives, or skills are the students learning in this lesson?

Genre

1. What genre will students use to complete this assignment?

2. Will the students choose their genres or will I assign them?

Time and Materials

1. How much time is needed for the assignment?

   _____ In class _____Out of class

2. What materials will students need for the assignment?

The assignment will be used as: *(Check all that apply)*

_____Grade _____Part of notes _____Journaling entry

_____Topic folder selection _____Portfolio entry _____For feedback

_____ Assignment to turn in _____Brainstorming ideas

_____ Other _____

B. *During Writing*

Flexible Grouping

Check all that apply:

_____Total group _____Alone _____Partner _____Small group

Notes for grouping students:_____

Revision will be included? ____Yes _____No

If yes, how? _____

Editing will be included? ____Yes   ____No

If yes, how? _____

The draft will be rewritten as a Neat Sheet? ____Yes ____No

C. *After Writing*

1. **Feedback**

    a. Who will provide the student with feedback on the activity? Check each space that applies:

        _____ Self ____ Teacher _____ Partner _____ Small group

    b. What form of feedback will be used?

        _____ Conference ____ Written comments _____ Rubrics

2. **Publishing**

    a. Will the writing be shared? _____ How? _____

    b. Will the assignment be published in a specific format or sequence? _____ Yes _____ No

    c. Will the work be displayed? _____ Yes _____ No

    How? _____ Where? _____

EFFECTIVE STUDENT AUTHORS IN THE DIFFERENTIATED CLASSROOM

> In a differentiated classroom, the teacher proactivity plans and carries out varied approaches to content, processs, and product in anticipation of and response to student differences in readiness, interest, and learning needs.
>
> —Tomlinson, 2001

A goal of teachers is to provide the guidance and support each student needs to become an effective author. Differentiated instruction provides student authors with an understanding of their thinking styles, their intelligences, and their personality profiles. Recognition of their strengths and genuine praise builds the young authors' confidence in their writing ability. They learn to view errors and weaknesses as opportunities to improve.

An effective author knows how to identify topics of interest and his most comfortable style for writing assignments and informal writing. He knows how to use his knowledge and related experiences in his writing. The productive young writer knows how to use various writing forms to communicate information he has learned. He possesses a repertoire of writing strategies he can apply automatically to organize and communicate his ideas. He knows he will not always "be there" with the reader, so he uses the skills in the writing craft to make the content clear and keep the reader's attention. He focuses on making his ideas clear. He lets the editor work with the mechanics.

The effective writer knows how to use the steps in the writing process. He realizes that revisions are always possible. He is aware that he may make many attempts before he produces a final copy. The young author's pride in his writing success is evident in his collection of notes, drafts, and final copies.

Internal motivation drives this author to succeed. He anticipates the rewards that come from audience appreciation and self-satisfaction. He knows that personal rewards come during and after writing. He looks forward to each writing experience as a self-fulfilling challenge.

The Rest of the Story . . .

Metamorphosis of Butterflies and Writers

When entering a flower garden, a visitor sees more butterflies if he moves quietly and looks carefully for the still, camouflaged creatures.

In the classroom, a teacher realizes the writing potential in young authors when he carefully and patiently observes and identifies the learners' various skills and abilities.

The release of butterflies brings delight to the beholder as the beautiful creatures spread their wings and take their individual flights.

When teachers develop effective authors, they know the students have communication tools for a lifetime of independent writing journeys.

REMEMBER!

Everyone is a writing teacher.
All students are writers.
Life is a journey of learning.

Always

Build confidence.
Nurture his uniqueness.
Cultivate his writing destiny.

References

Atwell, Nancie. (1998). *In the middle: New understandings about writing, reading, and learning.* Portsmouth, NH: Boynton/Cook.

Benton, S. I. (1997). Psychological foundations of elementary writing instruction. In G. D. Phye (Ed.), *Handbook of academic learning: Construction of knowledge.* San Diego, CA: Academic Press.

Brownjohn, Sandy. (1997). The Write Expression. *Times* educational supplement, April: 6.

Caine, R. N., & Caine, G. (1994). *Making connections: Teaching and the human brain.* Menlo Park, CA: Innovative Learning Publications.

Calkin, Lucy McCormick. (1994). *The art of teaching writing.* Portsmouth, NH: Heinemann.

Chamblee, Cynthia M. (1998). Bringing life to reading and writing for at risk college students. *Journal of Adolescent and Adult Literacy, 41,* April: 532.

Chapman, Carolyn. (1993). *If the shoe fits . . . How to develop multiple intelligences in the classroom.* Arlington Heights, IL: SkyLight.

Chapman, C., & Freeman, L. (1994). *Multiple intelligences through centers and projects.* Arlington Heights, IL: SkyLight.

Chapman, C., & King, R. (2000). *Test success in the brain compatible classroom.* Tucson, AZ: Zephyr Press.

Chapman, C., & King, R. (2003). *Differentiated instructional strategies for reading in the content areas.* Thousand Oaks, CA: Corwin Press.

Cleiman, Jennifer L. (1997). It takes a lot of bad writing. *Reading Teacher, 50,* April: 608.

Csikszentmihalyi, M. (1990). *Flow.* New York: Harper and Row.

Daiute, C., & Dalton, B. (1993). Collaboration between children learning to write: Can novices be masters? *Cognition and Instruction 10,* 281–333.

Englert, Carol Sue, Raphael, Taffy E., & Anderson, Linda M. (1992). Socially mediated instruction: improving students' knowledge and talk about writing. *Elementary School Journal, 92,* March: 411.

Ferrari, M., & Sternberg, R. J. (1998). *Self-awareness.* New York: Guilford.

Fisher, P. J. (1998). Teaching vocabulary in linguistically diverse classrooms. *Illinois Reading Council Journal, 26,* 16–21.

Fletcher, Ralph. (1993). *What a writer needs.* Portsmouth, NH: Heinemann.

Fletcher, R., & Portalupi, R. (1998). Craft lessons: Teaching writing K–8. Portland, ME: Stenhouse Publishers.

Frank, Marjorie. (1995). *If you're trying to teach kids how to write . . . You've gotta have this book.* Nashville, TN: Incentive Publications.

Fry, Don. (1996). Coaching at the center of the writing process. *American Editor.* December: 25.

Graves, Donald. (1990). Creating the writing room. *Instructor, 105,* October: 34.

Graves, Donald. (1999). *Bring life into learning: Create a lasting literacy.* Portsmouth, NH: Heinemann.

Gregory, Gayle, & Chapman, C. (2001). *Differentiated instructional strategies: One size doesn't fit all.* Thousand Oaks, CA: Corwin Press, Inc.

Keil, F. (1999). Cognition. In M. Bennett (Ed.), *Developmental psychology: Achievements and prospects.* Philadelphia: Psychology Press.

Kemper, Dave, Sebranek, P., & Meyer, V. (1998). *All write: A handbook for writing and learning.* Wilmington, MA: Great Source Education Group, Inc.

Kendrick, Shirley, & Forler, Nan. (1997). The writers' group. *Reading Teacher, 51,* September: 79.

Lane, Barry. (1993). *After the end: Teaching and learning creative revision.* Portsmouth, NH: Heinemann.

Lipsitz, J. (1984). *Successful schools for young adolescents.* New Brunswick, NJ: Transaction Books.

Martin, Steve. (1996). Writing is easy. *New Yorker, 72,* June: 156.

Mayer, Jennifer. (1996). Assessing student thinking through writing. *Mathematics Teacher, 8,* May: 428.

McGinley, W. J., & Denner, P. R. (1987). Story impressions: A prereading/writing activity. *Journal of Reading, 31,* 248–253.

Piaget, J. (1952). *The origins of intelligence in children.* New York: International Universities Press.

Pintrich, P. R., & Schunk, D. H. (1996). *Motivation in education: Theory, research, and application.* Upper Saddle River, NJ: Merrill/Prentice Hall.

Poindexter, Candace C., & Oliver, Irene R. (1998). Producing classroom writing. *Reading Teacher, 52,* December: 420.

Raines, Peggy A. (1996). Writing portfolios: Turning the house into a home. *English Journal, 85,* January: 41.

Ray, Katie Wood. (1999). *Wondrous words: Writers and writing in the elementary classroom.* Urbana, IL: National Council of Teachers of English.

Renzulli, Joseph S., & Reis, Sally M. (1998). Talent development through curriculum differentiation. *NAASP Bulletin, 82,* February: 6.

Santrock, John W. (2001) *Educational psychology.* New York: McGraw Hill.

Schunk, D. H. (1996). *Learning theories* (2nd ed.). Upper Saddle River, NJ: Merrill/Prentice Hall.

Senatra, Richard. (2000). Teaching learners to think, read and write more effectively in content subjects. *Clearing House, 73,* May: 266.

Sexton, Melissa, Harris, Karen, & Graham, Steve. (1998). Self-regulated strategy development and the writing process and the effects on essay writing and attributions. *Exceptional Children 64,* Spring: 295.

Siegler, R. S. (1998). *Children's thinking* (3rd ed.). Upper Saddle River, NJ: Erlbaum.

Sousa, David. (2001). *How the brain learns.* Thousand Oaks, CA: Corwin Press.

Stipek, D. (1998). *Motivation to learn: From theory to practice.* Boston: Allyn and Bacon.

Stipek, D. J. (1996). Motivation and instruction. In D. C. Berliner & R. C. Calfee (Eds.), *Handbook of educational psychology*. New York: Macmillan.

Tomlinson (2001). How to differentiate instruction in mixed-ability classrooms. (2nd ed.). Alexandria, VA: Association for Supervision and Curriculum Development.

Van, Horn, Leigh. (1997). The characters within us: Readers connect with characters to create meaning and understanding. *Journal of Adolescence and Adult Literacy*. February: 342.

Zimmerman, B. J., Bandura, A., & Martinez-Pons, M. (1992). Self-motivation for academic attainment. The role of self-efficacy beliefs and personal goal setting. *American Educational Research Journal, 29*, 663–676.

Zimmerman, B. J., Bonner, S., & Kovach, R. (1996). *Developing self-regulated learners*. Washington, DC: American Psychological Association.

Index

**CORWIN
PRESS**

The Corwin Press logo—a raven striding across an open book—represents the happy union of courage and learning. We are a professional-level publisher of books and journals for K-12 educators, and we are committed to creating and providing resources that embody these qualities. Corwin's motto is "Success for All Learners."